KIDS IN COURT

THE ACLU DEFENDS THEIR RIGHTS

by Sam and Beryl Epstein

FOUR WINDS PRESS   NEW YORK

LIBRARY OF CONGRESS CATALOGING IN PUBLICATION DATA

Epstein, Sam (date)
  Kids in court.

  Includes bibliographical references and index.
  Summary: Examines cases involving young people in which
the American Civil Liberties Union felt civil rights, guaran-
teed by the Constitution, had been denied.
    1. Students—Legal status, laws, etc.—United States—
Juvenile literature. 2. Children—Legal status, laws,
etc.—United States—Juvenile literature. 3. American Civil
Liberties Union—Juvenile literature. [1. Civil rights—
Cases. 2. Children's rights. 3. American Civil Liberties
Union] I. Epstein, Beryl Williams (date). II. Title.
KF4150.Z9E67   344.73′079   81-69515
  ISBN 0-590-07669-8   347.30479   AACR2

PUBLISHED BY FOUR WINDS PRESS

A DIVISION OF SCHOLASTIC INC., NEW YORK, N.Y.

PRINTED IN THE UNITED STATES OF AMERICA

LIBRARY OF CONGRESS CATALOG CARD NUMBER: 81-69515

1 2 3 4 5 86 85 84 83 82

ACKNOWLEDGMENTS

Among the many people who helped us with this book we are especially indebted to Roger Baldwin (1884–1981), founder of the ACLU; to Alan Reitman, Associate Director, Frank Askin, General Counsel, and Trudi Schutz, Information Director, all of that organization; to Gara La-Marche, Assistant Director, and Richard Emery, Staff Attorney, of the NYCLU; Amelia D. Lewis of Sun City, Arizona; Hilda Silverman, Executive Director, ACLU Greater Philadelphia Branch; Spencer Coxe, Philadelphia, Pennsylvania; Judah Labovitz, New York, New York; Mary Weidler, Executive Director, Alabama CLU; Morris Dees, Montgomery, Alabama; Stephen M. Nagler, former Executive Director, ACLU of New Jersey; Louis Lusky, Columbia University School of Law, New York; Irwin A. Hyman, Temple University, Philadelphia; Joseph J. Snellenburg II, judge of the Family Court of the State of New York, Suffolk County; and Beverly Reingold, our editor.

CONTENTS

1

About the ACLU

This is a book of case histories. It reports the factual stories of young people who, in the opinion of the ACLU—the American Civil Liberties Union—were denied the civil rights guaranteed to all Americans by the Constitution of the United States. (Until the 1960s, young people were not generally regarded as entitled to claim those rights.) The ACLU was involved in all these cases. In each one it challenged some form of government—local police, a county sheriff, a school board, a state or federal agency. It did so because, as Roger Baldwin, the ACLU's founder, once put it, "Our job is to protect citizens from the abuse of their rights by the government."

The term *civil rights*, it should perhaps be noted, has become popularly identified during the past few decades with efforts to protect minorities from various forms of discrimination based on race, creed, sex, or color. It has thus come to represent, in the minds of many people, only rights such as nondiscriminatory housing, education, employment, and the use of such public facilities as theaters, restaurants, hotels, parks, and swimming pools. In this book the term is used in its original and larger sense, to represent not only those rights but all the rights spelled out in the Constitution's first ten amendments, known as the Bill of Rights, and in certain later amendments. They include, among others, the rights of free speech, press, religion, assembly, and association; the right to a fair and speedy trial; the right to be protected against cruel and unusual punishment.

What then about the term *civil liberties*, as used in the ACLU's name? The two terms, *civil rights* and *civil liberties*, are often used interchangeably, but Roger Baldwin did distinguish between the two. He put it like this: Civil *rights* are those spelled out by the Constitution's amendments; civil *liberties*, based on principles expressed by those amendments, become legal rights only when they are embodied in "enforceable law," such as a legislative act or a judicial decision.

Some of the cases in this book have been called landmarks in the history of the law, because they mark important developments in the interpretation of our Constitution. They have helped express constitutional principles in a new form of legally protected civil rights.

But before we get down to those cases, it seems important to say something about the ACLU itself: what it is, how it came into existence, how it has survived, and how it has affected the changing times of the twentieth century.

The ACLU has been involved in controversy since the moment of its birth in 1920. Because civil rights are always under attack somewhere or other in the United States, the ACLU is always engaged in argument and—where argument fails—in legal action. If it loses one battle, it doesn't retire in peace; instead, it actively seeks a reason for starting another on the same or similar grounds. Even when it is victorious, as it often is, its victories are so likely to be challenged that they must—if they are to have any permanent effect—be won again, sometimes again and again.

But the ACLU itself is also a subject of controversy. There are those who praise it enthusiastically as the steadfast champion of the Constitution. There are others who regard it indignantly as a meddlesome, troublemaking organization, chipping away at the foundations of our system of government. There are still others who find it positively alarming because the rights it defends include, as Baldwin has pointed out, "the rights of the sons-of-bitches."

Even members of the ACLU, those people all over the country who support it with their dues and in many instances with their tireless volunteer service, sometimes abandon it in disappointment or anger. They may be disappointed because it has failed to take up the cudgels for what they see as a worthy cause. They may be angry because it has taken a stand they can't agree with—a stand, say, defending freedom of speech for Communists or freedom of assembly for the American Nazi Party. But most members do persist in their support, and many have done so for decades.

The ACLU's founder, Roger Nash Baldwin, served as its director for its first thirty years. Thereafter he was a member of its National Advisory Council, and served as adviser to its international program, until his retirement in 1981—two years after the ACLU had marked his ninety-fifth birthday with a gala celebration. During all those years the ACLU's program was largely a reflection of his ideas, and the organization's development into a powerful defender of Americans' civil rights came about mainly through his unique abilities.

Baldwin was born in 1884. He was the oldest of six children who grew up in a large, servant-staffed house in Wellesley, Massachusetts, Boston's neighbor. Both his parents could trace their families back to English immigrants who had sailed for the New World aboard the *Mayflower*. Baldwin's father was a well-to-do manufacturer. One of his uncles was president of a railroad. Roger Baldwin went to Harvard as a matter of course, showing scant evidence of the "radical" ideas for which he would later, on more than one occasion, find himself behind bars. But even the young Baldwin felt strongly that, as he always put it, "you had to help the underdog."

He finished college in three years and then remained at Harvard for a fourth year to take a master's degree in the burgeoning new science of anthropology. Shortly afterward he left for St. Louis, Missouri, where he spent the next eleven years. Everything he did there helped transform the naïve, well-meaning young man into one remarkably equipped to initiate and guide the ACLU.

The reason Roger Baldwin went to St. Louis was to serve as director of Self Culture Hall, a settlement house devoted to the needs of recent German and Irish immigrants. Whenever police apprehended any of the neighborhood's boys for fighting or stealing, Baldwin went with them to court to look after their interests. Through these experiences he became familiar with the city's special court for juveniles.

Juvenile courts were still new in that first decade of the twentieth century. But already they were changing the age-old custom of trying juvenile offenders in criminal courts, where adult lawbreakers were tried. For hundreds of years criminal courts had sentenced even young children to prison, along with hardened criminals, or on occasion had them put to death. Then, from the early nineteenth century on, they had sentenced them for months, sometimes for years, to institutions known as reform schools or industrial training schools. But whatever sentence criminal courts had given young offenders, their purpose was always the same: to punish them for wrongdoing. The purpose of a juvenile court, on the other hand, was to rehabilitate the young.

Baldwin learned that the judge of a juvenile court was expected to serve *in loco parentis*—in place of a parent. For each case the judge set up a special rehabilitation process. Usually it required that a child be supervised for a specific period of time by one of the court's special staff of probation officers. Each of those officers, like the judge himself, was expected to have the child's best interests at heart. And the juvenile court judge enlisted the help of schools, churches, and various community groups to bolster the probation officers' efforts.

Baldwin fought hard to win public support for the court's rehabilitation program. He was so effective that the judge asked him to serve as his probation chief. Baldwin then formed the local Probation Officers Association, the first of its kind. Eventually it grew into the National Conference on Crime and Delinquency.

Leaving St. Louis for a summer, Baldwin took Harvard's

pioneering course in sociology. When he returned to St. Louis, he taught the first sociology course ever offered by Washington University—at the same time continuing his work as probation chief and, for a while longer, as settlement house director. With his young college students he visited police courts and hospitals for the poor, and explored the areas of the city given over to prostitution, gambling, and the sale of opium. The idea of social work as a profession—an idea Baldwin was introducing to his students—was also new. And the Social Service Conference he organized, which brought professional skills to help solve the city's social problems, was another historic first.

Soon Roger Baldwin's various achievements had earned him wide recognition, and he was being sought for jobs in Boston, New York, Washington, and other cities. One well-known social worker recommended him for a government post in Washington as "a man of unusual ability and power to conciliate and persuade people of many different kinds and dispositions."

Baldwin turned down each offer until St. Louis's Civic League, which he had joined as soon as he moved to the city, asked him to serve as its secretary, or working director. He accepted, and on a full-time basis, because the job gave him, he said, "the chance to experiment with changes in the democratic form of government."

Under his leadership the league won acceptance of the progressive city charter it had long been working for, against the opposition of local politicians and other strongly entrenched groups. During Baldwin's tenure, the league also undertook the reorganization of the city's agencies dealing with children. And it brought a suit to allow blacks to own property anywhere in St. Louis, rather than only in specified areas.

That last battle was not won until it reached the United

States Supreme Court. From then on, Baldwin said later, "I placed my faith in the courts."

In the meantime, on his own, Baldwin became involved with the IWW, the pioneering labor organization properly known as the International Workers of the World. Each winter hundreds of its members, commonly called Wobblies, appeared in St. Louis. They had worked as farm laborers during the harvest season and would not work again until spring planting time. Homeless and destitute, they were arrested as vagrants or for walking out of restaurants without paying their bills. The Wobblies had a reputation for violence, but Baldwin found them "serious and clean and fraternal—completely in the spirit of the American frontier independence." To provide them with free food and shelter, he created the city's first municipal lodgings. His belief in the rights of workers to a decent life was one more conviction Baldwin would act upon as director of the ACLU.

During his years in St. Louis, Roger Baldwin came to know many of the most famous people of the day. Some he met during his frequent travels. Others accepted his invitation to speak before the influential and civic-minded St. Louis City Club, one more organization Baldwin had founded. Among these people were Theodore Roosevelt, Woodrow Wilson, and Margaret Sanger, America's first courageous leader of the birth-control movement. But the person who most influenced his thinking during this time was Emma Goldman, the famous Russian-born anarchist.

Baldwin had to be dared into attending the meeting where he first heard a speech by the "Red Queen of Anarchy," as Goldman was called. To him, as to most Americans, she had seemed a frighteningly dangerous revolutionary. But, as he listened to her, he decided that what she was saying made "plain good sense." It seemed to him that she stood, quite simply, for freedom from all forms of coercion, and that was close to his own New England–nourished philosophy of resistance to tyranny. Baldwin later gave a party in Emma Goldman's honor at St. Louis's best hotel. Although it raised a good many eyebrows, Baldwin was unfazed. He would remain the anarchist's lifelong friend.

Like most of his countrymen, Baldwin was stunned by the 1914 outbreak of war in Europe. He immediately joined the new American Union Against Militarism, founded by a group of highly respected pacifists. Its goal was a swift and honorable peace brought about through negotiations it hoped the United States would initiate. Baldwin became its St. Louis representative.

But peace seemed increasingly remote as the war went on. Soon Baldwin was reading about young Englishmen who were taking their own kind of stand against it: They were refusing to fight. Their conscience would not permit them, they said, to kill other human beings. Those British conscientious objectors, as they called themselves, were denounced on both sides of the Atlantic as cowards or traitors. To Baldwin, however, they appeared to have the courage and wisdom that could point the way to a world without war. He decided that if he were called upon to fight, he would do exactly as they were doing.

In the spring of 1917, with the war still devastating Europe and both opposing forces trying to win the United States as an ally, Baldwin left St. Louis for New York. There, on April 2, he volunteered his services full-time to the American Union Against Militarism.

Four days later the United States entered the war as an ally of England and France against their German foe. Baldwin assumed the overwhelming task of providing legal defense for those who were suddenly being publicly humiliated or arrested for their "unpatriotic" opposition to the military draft and all new wartime regulations. To keep this work from interfering with the union's program, which was still concerned specifically with bringing about a negotiated peace, he carried it on through the subsidiary organization he set up. Originally called the Bureau for Conscientious Objectors, it was later renamed the National Civil Liberties Bureau.

Some months later, after several important union members had objected to the new bureau's existence, the National Civil Liberties Bureau became a completely independent organization. Baldwin, two young lawyers who shared his convictions, one paid secretary, and occasional part-time volunteers made up its staff.

Traveling back and forth between New York and Washington, where the bureau also set up an office, Baldwin regularly called on the secretary of war and other government officials. Many of them, whom he already knew, sympathized with his aim of developing legal formulas to protect people still opposed to the war or to military service in it. Thanks to their help, the bureau was able to provide sound advice to men of draft age. Those who could defend a claim to conscientious objection to killing, for example, were told of their legal right to work on a farm instead, or to perform some other equally vital wartime service.

But many people accused the bureau of deliberately encouraging men to become slackers, or draft dodgers, as conscientious objectors were often scornfully called. If that charge could be proved, the bureau's staff would be guilty of treason under a new Espionage Act. Seeking to prove its guilt, half a dozen federal officers, enthusiastically assisted by nearly twice that many volunteer patriots, raided the bureau's office on a Saturday morning in August 1918. The raiding party left with all of the bureau's files.

Less than two weeks later Baldwin himself was called to register for military service. He wrote his draft board immediately. "I am opposed to the use of force to accomplish any ends, however good," his letter explained. "I am, therefore, opposed . . . not only to direct military service, but to any service whatever designed to help the war." And it ended, in words Emma Goldman herself might have dictated, with: "I will decline to perform any service under compulsion, regardless of its character."

On October 9, having been ordered to report for his physical examination, Baldwin replied that he "respectfully" declined to appear. A day or so later a plainclothesman arrived to conduct him to his draft board, whose chairman suggested that Baldwin spend the night in jail to reconsider his position. Baldwin did spend the night in a cold, dark cell furnished with only a wooden bench and a bucket. But the next day, as planned, he pleaded guilty to willful violation of the draft law. The judge sentenced him to prison, and he was taken to New York's big, gloomy Tombs.

The following morning, to his surprise, he was turned over to the custody of a marshall, who delivered him to an office of the Justice Department. There—ACLU members still like to repeat this story—he was asked to reorganize his bureau's files. The eager patriots who had participated in the office raid had left them in such disorder that the Justice Department staff couldn't discover whether or not they showed evidence of Espionage Act violation.

During the month in which Baldwin worked daily on the files—they proved the bureau's innocence, as he had known they would—he was treated as an honored guest. And the marshall who accompanied him back and forth from prison each day became such a good friend that he once took Baldwin to a burlesque show before returning him to the Tombs that night.

The armistice that ended the war had no effect on the prison terms of draft-law violators. The very day it was signed—November 11, 1918—Baldwin was transferred to a penitentiary in New Jersey. There, to no one's surprise, he quite enjoyed serving out the rest of his year's sentence, minus the usual two months for good behavior. He worked in the prison kitchen. He set up classes for the inmates. He formed a glee club. He persuaded the public library to open a branch within the walls. He hired a good lawyer—whose fees were provided by the high-stakes gamblers among his fellow prisoners—to advise men who hoped to appeal what they saw as unfair convictions or who sought help on other legal matters.

After his release Baldwin returned to a bureau that had been faltering without his energetic presence. There was plenty of work to be done; many men and women were still being penalized for their antiwar activities. But Baldwin had been thinking about another organization, one that could serve more broadly as "watchdog for the underdog," as he liked to put it, or "watchdog for civil liberties." He saw the need for an organization pledged to defend the right of dissent wherever it was threatened, and also to defend the rights of workers. Workers, Baldwin felt, were the Americans whose rights were then being "most attacked."

Those who had faithfully supported the bureau now approved of Baldwin's new and wider purpose. They closed the bureau and, on January 20, 1920, founded the American Civil Liberties Union.

Sixty-four prominent Americans, many of them Baldwin's personal friends, accepted his invitation to serve as the ACLU's first national board. Among them were clergymen, educators, writers, political leaders, leaders of the rising labor movement, and such courageous lawyers as the already well known Felix Frankfurter, who would one day sit on the bench of the Supreme Court. The ACLU's headquarters were a few rooms in what had once been a private house in New York's Greenwich Village. The staff consisted of Baldwin himself, two full-time associates, and a lawyer serving as the ACLU's part-time counsel. Their salaries were paid (Baldwin received $125 a month) and their activities supported by the few thousand people throughout the country who were willing to pay dues to an organization generally suspected of radicalism.

That first small New York office was busy from the moment of its opening, constantly answering questions from people seeking legal advice or help. Nevertheless, its staff frequently went out seeking work, so to speak. As Baldwin explained it, "We were always provoking cases one way or another, by sending our people into places where there had been a denial of the right to talk, and getting them arrested purposely, in order to test whether those bans were legal."

Test cases, still made use of by the ACLU today, have almost always had to do with the widespread denial of rights common to a particular period. During the twenties, for example, in the wake of the 1918 Russian Revolution, fear of a Communist uprising in the United States resulted in denial of the civil rights of American Communists and others who could be labeled "Red" in the hysteria of the time. Police banned meetings of political radicals or arrested those attending them. An Episcopal bishop, volunteering for an ACLU test case of Communists' rights to free speech and assembly, was arrested for attending a New Jersey Communists' meeting that the police had officially banned. Baldwin made sure the press was on hand for the arrest and for the bishop's later release. Publicity is a tool the ACLU has always known how to use for the protection of civil liberties and for furthering the public's education in the need for their defense.

And the twenties, of course, also saw the wide denial of workers' rights that Baldwin had recognized. The workers then involved in labor union organization were countering the opposition of their bosses with protest meetings, protest marches, and strikes, and those activities brought them into frequent conflict with the law. Baldwin himself was arrested during a strike of silk-mill workers in Paterson, New Jersey, although that occasion didn't grow out of a test case. The ACLU had been asked for assistance by striking workers whose use of a hall, where they had been meeting peacefully, was suddenly banned by the police.

Baldwin found another hall that he was told would be open to the strikers, but when he went there with them, he saw that its entrance was blocked by club-bearing police. Baldwin and five union leaders, carrying an American flag and a copy of the Constitution, then led a protest march to City Hall. The six men had just mounted an improvised platform, with the intention of reading aloud the Bill of Rights, when the crowd gathered around them was charged by police. The strikers fled under flailing clubs. Baldwin and the other five men were arrested and taken to court.

Freed on bail shortly afterward, Baldwin promptly scheduled another meeting for the strikers and announced to the press the names of the well-known people who would attend it as the strikers' guests. The prominence of these guests had the influence Baldwin had hoped for. That meeting took place in the same hall to which the police had previously barred entrance.

Within a few weeks the strike was settled. But on the day the silk-mill workers returned to their jobs, Baldwin and the five strike leaders—who had all remained free on bail until then—were indicted for unlawful assembly under a 1796 state statute. The strike leaders were fined $50 each and Baldwin was sentenced to six months in jail. The ACLU appealed the verdict, and eventually it was reversed by New Jersey's highest court. That court's judge declared that ancient law could not be made use of to prevent people from doing anything they had a right to do under the Constitution—and the Constitution guaranteed them the right to assemble peaceably.

In 1935, when a decision of the U.S. Supreme Court upheld the new National Labor Relations Act, workers were assured the right to bargain collectively. Overnight, it seemed, the tide that had run against labor for so long had been reversed. Henry Ford, millionaire industrialist, employer of thousands of auto workers and an open enemy of unions, was found guilty of unfair labor practices. The National Labor Relations Board ordered him to stop firing or threatening to fire any employee who joined the United Auto Workers Union. He was also ordered to stop distributing in his factories leaflets critical of the union.

The ACLU quickly got involved in the much-talked-of Ford case. But members of the board were split over the stand the organization should take. One faction felt that Henry Ford was as entitled to free speech as his workers and should be permitted to continue his antiunion campaign unhampered. The other faction felt the charge against Ford was justified—that the right to free speech did not give an employer the right to threaten his employees. The compromise the two factions finally agreed on was the one accepted by the Supreme Court for the settlement of the case: Ford did not have the right to threaten his workers with loss of their jobs if they joined a union, but he did have the right to voice his antiunion opinions.

Workers' newly guaranteed right to collective bargaining meant that the ACLU would no longer be as active as it had been in workers' defense cases. The National Labor Relations Act and other legislation passed during Franklin D. Roosevelt's New Deal of the thirties were part of what Baldwin referred to in his 1970 report of the ACLU's first fifty years. In that half century, he declared, the United States had "witnessed the most remarkable growth of law to protect the rights of citizens in all its history."

Some of the new laws and regulations Baldwin was writing of had resulted from ACLU court victories. Some were passed with the assistance of the ACLU's lobbying program, developed during the 1950s to promote civil rights legislation by working with congressmen and members of state legislatures.

After Baldwin's retirement as its director in 1950, the ACLU's New York-based board of directors decided it was necessary to broaden the organization that had originated as a small group of Baldwin's dedicated friends. The ACLU, the board members agreed, should have affiliates, or chapters, in every state—if possible, in every community. Its members would then be alert to civil-rights violations wherever they occurred, and would stand ready to oppose them.

Baldwin's successors carried out that plan, and within a few short years the ACLU was growing in leaps and bounds. By 1962 it had thirty-one affiliates; by 1970 it had forty-eight. Today, with an annual budget of close to $5 million, it has three regional offices, fifty state affiliates (with slightly varying names, such as the ACLU of Oregon and the Arizona CLU), and about 400 local chapters. Its membership nationwide is about 200,000, and its paid staff about 200. Some 3,000 persons serve as leaders on its boards and committees, and as its cooperating attorneys—that is, as lawyers who, without fee, carry out much of the legal work on the 6,000 cases it handles annually. Funds for much of its activity, since 1966, come from the ACLU Foundation. Members of the ACLU's executive committee serve as the foundation's board, and the ACLU's staff helps administer its program. But because the foundation was incorporated under a law permitting contributions to educational and charitable institutions to be exempt from taxation, it has been able to raise large sums for the ACLU's legal and public education work.

The new direction the ACLU was able to take, from the 1960s on, was clearly expressed by Aryeh Neier, who became its executive director in 1970. Neier had already served as the ACLU's field director, providing valuable support to Martin Luther King's civil rights movement. Like Ira Glasser, who succeeded him as director in 1978, Neier took exception to calling the ACLU a "watchdog," as Baldwin had often done. "Being a watchdog is sitting back and waiting for some intruder to violate someone's civil liberties," he said. "We have to be a good deal of a hounddog."

"We're not just interested in seeing to it that rights are not abused," Neier further pointed out. "We want to see a society in which people use their rights."

Various grants and bequests now help support the many special programs the ACLU is involved in, all aimed at urging people to know their rights and to use them. They include the National Coalition Against Censorship, the Capital Punishment Project, the Women's Rights and Children's Rights projects. And its numerous publications now include a series of paperback books, each spelling out the rights that a specific group of people may demand and use. Among the groups the books address are students, young people, parents, teachers, prisoners, the mentally retarded, aliens, and police officers.

The ACLU's criteria for deciding to tackle a case have not changed over the years, either for the national office or for its affiliates, all of which can and do take up cases on their own. An alleged violation of rights must pass one of three tests to qualify for ACLU intervention:

1. Has freedom of inquiry or expression been violated?
2. Is due process of law affected? (Due process provides an accused person such rights as the right to counsel, the right to confront and cross-examine accusers, the right to remain silent.)
3. Has there been discrimination based on race, color, sex, or national origin?

The only other criterion the ACLU considers, before taking a case, is whether winning it could result in the improvement or abolishment of a law that it regards as restricting civil rights.

It should be mentioned here that the ACLU does not always fight a case on its own. It often cooperates with other organizations or individuals who are bringing into court a case that meets the ACLU's criteria. Then it may simply state its position by offering the court a brief, called an *amicus curiae* brief. The Latin words mean friend of the court.

The ACLU has now participated, in one role or another, in many thousands of cases. The few additional cases that can be mentioned in this chapter are among the most significant. Some are from its earliest days. Others are more recent.

In the 1920s the ACLU fought a case that may sound

almost unbelievable today, when sex manuals are openly displayed in drugstores and on supermarket racks. It fought a decision by the federal Customs Bureau that *Married Love,* a book of advice on marital relations by an eminent British scientist, was unfit for Americans to read and could not be imported into the United States. The Customs Bureau of that time had a great deal to say about which books and works of art were allowed to cross our borders. But its power of censorship was considerably diminished by this case, recorded in court papers as *The United States* v. *Married Love.* (The one-letter abbreviation stands for *versus,* Latin for against.) Love and the ACLU were triumphant. The Customs Bureau was ordered to permit the book's entry.

In 1925 the ACLU decided to provoke a case testing the constitutionality of a new Tennessee law. The law stated that only the biblical story of creation could be taught in the public schools to explain the presence of human beings on earth. In other words, it outlawed the teaching of the Darwinian theory of evolution. The ACLU's board members felt the law could be challenged as a violation of the constitutional separation of church and state, and also because it violated teachers' right to free speech and the cherished concept of academic freedom. So the board issued a statement to the press offering the legal services of the ACLU to any Tennessee teacher accused of breaking the new law.

Shortly afterward the ACLU received a telegram stating that John Thomas Scopes, a young science teacher in Dayton, Tennessee, would provide the ACLU with its test case by continuing to teach evolution in his classes. Scopes kept his word and was promptly arrested. The ACLU filed suit against the State of Tennessee.

Before a lawyer could be invited to represent Scopes, one of the most outstanding men in the country offered to assist Tennessee's state attorney in Scopes's prosecution. He was William Jennings Bryan, three-time presidential candidate. Famed as a "silver-tongued" orator, Bryan was a fervent defender of the literal truth of every word in the Bible. The announcement of his role in the case caused another famous man of the time, Clarence Darrow, criminal lawyer and staunch agnostic, to volunteer as Scopes's defender. The ACLU's board probably would have preferred a less flamboyant representative and one better versed in constitutional law. It couldn't refuse a man of Darrow's stature, however, so it accepted his offer and provided him with a battery of constitutional lawyers to serve as his assistants.

The trial became a circus. The little town of Dayton, sweltering in the summer heat, was overrun with photographers, reporters, and sightseers. Everyone wanted to watch and listen to Bryan and Darrow, both in shirt sleeves and galluses, cooling themselves with palmetto fans as they matched each other's "matchless" rhetoric. The constitutional questions—sometimes even Scopes himself—were forgotten as the men argued what Baldwin described as the case of "the Good Book against Darwin, bigotry against science, or . . . God against the monkeys."

The jury deliberated just nine minutes. Scopes was found guilty and fined $100. The ACLU immediately appealed to the Tennessee Supreme Court, assuming it would lose again there and could then take the case on to the Supreme Court of the United States.

The judges of the higher Tennessee court did agree with the lower court's decision. That much is clear from their opinions. But because they didn't want their state law tested by the U.S. Supreme Court, they found a way to end the case then and there. Making use of a technicality—the Dayton judge had himself imposed the fine on Scopes, rather than leaving that task to the jury, as he should have done—the Tennessee Supreme Court reversed Scopes's conviction. The ACLU thus had no basis for taking the case to the nation's highest court, and the antievolution law remained in force in Tennessee.

That Supreme Court decision indicated that the justices had avoided the "difficult terrain" of a teacher's academic freedom. They were, in other words, leaving unsettled the question of whether or not a teacher was, as Bryan had insisted, a "hired man" who "cannot demand a salary for saying what his employers do not want said."

Nevertheless, the "monkey trial," as it is usually called, raised so much furor and spawned so many jokes and cartoons that a number of other states shied away from passing laws similar to Tennessee's. An antievolution statute that Arkansas did put on its books was challenged by a case that reached the U.S. Supreme Court in 1968. There the statute was declared unconstitutional on the grounds that it had been passed for religious reasons and therefore conflicted with the First Amendment: "Congress shall make no law respecting an establishment of religion."

Then, in 1981, religious fundamentalists sharing Bryan's views about the Bible won passage, in Arkansas and Louisiana, of laws requiring "balanced" classroom teaching of evolution and what they call "creation science." The ACLU's swift challenge of the Arkansas law won a January, 1982, decision, in a U.S. district court, that "creation science" was not a science at all. Arkansas law, Judge William Law Overton ruled, was "simply and purely an effort to introduce the biblical version of creation into the public school curricula," and was unconstitutional. This decision's effect on the ACLU's challenge of the Louisiana law, and on the passage of similar laws in other states, still remains to be seen.

The use of prayer in schools has also been—and continues to be—the cause of lawsuits. In 1962, for example, five parents of students in a New York State public school brought an ACLU-supported suit against the school's board of education. That suit challenged the board's order that at the start of each school day the students recite a nonsectarian prayer generally known as "the Regents' Prayer." The order had been adopted on the recommendation of the state's Board of Regents, which has wide powers over New York's educational system. In 1963 the suit reached the U.S. Supreme Court, where a six-to-one decision held that the prayer be dropped because its use violated the First Amendment.

Many Protestant and most Jewish religious leaders approved that decision, but there was an immediate outcry against it from other Protestant clergymen and from Catholic leaders generally. The ACLU reacted the way it often does at the announcement of an important verdict by the Supreme Court: It called the decision to the attention of its affiliates. In that particular communication it suggested that the affiliates monitor the public schools in their area to find out if they were following any "illegal" religious practices.

Laws are currently being tested, or remain to be tested, that attempt to circumvent the decision against the Regents' Prayer. One, in Louisiana, allows school boards to institute daily prayers. Another, in Massachusetts, requires a daily school period of silent prayer or meditation. That law was passed after one allowing voluntary prayers in school had been declared unconstitutional by the state's Supreme Court in 1980.

All such laws recall a 1947 statement by U.S. Supreme

Court Justice Wiley B. Rutledge. There were, he wrote, "two great drives . . . in the name of education" to abridge the Constitution's complete division of church and state. One was "to introduce religious education and observances into public schools." The other was "to obtain public funds for aid and support of various private religious schools."

The ACLU's stand on those two drives has already been made clear. The organization is flatly opposed to all religious education and observance in public schools. Its opinion is divided as to the use of public funds for private religious schools. It opposes the use of tax money for, among other things, their teachers' salaries, the purchase of their textbooks and equipment, and the transportation of their students. But the ACLU does not object to the use of public tax money to help private schools provide noneducational services to children—services that are normally provided by a community in its concern for the safety and physical welfare of its school children. Such services include physical, dental, and psychological examinations, and hot school lunches.

In another group of cases having to do with religion, the ACLU has defended a different constitutional right also guaranteed by the First Amendment: the right to religious freedom. In some of the most famous of these cases it brought suits, or joined in suits, on behalf of the sect known as Jehovah's Witnesses.

Jehovah's Witnesses believe they must worship no earthly images, but only God Himself. And since they regard a flag as an earthly image, they don't allow their children to "worship" it with a salute or a pledge of allegiance. As a result, in the early thirties, some two thousand of their children were expelled from various public schools throughout the country.

One suit to have those children readmitted was brought against a Pennsylvania board of education. After an eight-year battle it reached the U.S. Supreme Court, where it lost the decision by an eight-to-one vote. Justice Felix Frankfurter, once a member of the ACLU's first board of directors, wrote the Court's opinion and thereby lost the friendship of Roger Baldwin for many years.

That decision distressed many other Americans as much as it did Baldwin. But some people, pleased by the decision, saw it as an excuse for acts of mob violence against the "unpatriotic" Jehovah's Witnesses. And it was the viciousness of their attacks that helped bring about a reconsideration of the decision.

Several members of the Supreme Court soon let it be known they felt they had been wrong in their vote on that case. And when a similar case was brought before the court in 1942, this one on behalf of children in West Virginia— it is known in law books as *West Virginia* v. *Barnette*— the earlier decision was reversed. The justices voted six to three that Jehovah's Witnesses should not be compelled to perform an act that was against the principles of their religion. To expel children from school for failing to salute or pledge allegiance to the flag, their majority opinion said, violated the First Amendment and was therefore prohibited.

It has been said that the ACLU, born in the aftermath of World War I, almost died during World War II. It didn't die, of course, but it did suffer from internal dissension that left it weakened for some time.

The first conflict arose before the United States entered the war, when the Soviet Union signed a nonaggression pact with Nazi Germany. That pact enabled Hitler to start his *blitzkrieg* against western Europe. And when the American Communist party supported the pact, despite widespread horror over Nazi atrocities, a wave of anticommunism arose in the United States. Communist meetings were harassed, party members lost their jobs, and in general their civil rights were threatened. The ACLU, true to its belief that no one should be persecuted because of unpopular political opinions, stepped in to defend those rights.

But certain of its influential members wanted to rid its board of Elizabeth Gurley Flynn, a Communist party leader. Flynn, also an outstanding labor leader and a member of the ACLU board since its inception, had offered to resign from the board when she joined the Communist party in 1938. At that time her offer had not been accepted. Now, however, the board asked for her resignation. The reason given was that an organization dedicated to defending civil liberties should not have, on its policy-making board, a member of the political party that openly supported a pact with Hitler. And when Flynn refused to resign, the board, after six hours of angry argument, decided by a one-vote margin to expel her.

Some of the ACLU's oldest and most illustrious members protested. Many asked how an organization that had always opposed discrimination against Communists for their political views could now exclude a Communist from its own board.

Flynn's expulsion remained a sore point within the organization until 1976. That year the ACLU officially declared that its board's decision had not been consistent with the ACLU's basic principles. Elizabeth Gurley Flynn's "good name" was restored in the annals of the organization, but many people still blamed the ACLU for what it had done to her.

There were also many ACLU members, and many outside the organization, who blamed it for what they felt it did *not* do during World War II. They said it did not make enough effort to defend the civil rights of the 112,000 residents of western coastal states who were sent to concentration camps after the attack on Pearl Harbor made Japan our enemy overnight. Two-thirds of those people, all of whom were of Japanese ancestry, were American citizens. None had been charged with a crime or tried in a court of law. But by a presidential proclamation of February 19, 1942, put into effect by military authorities, all were evacuated from homes they were forced to leave unguarded or sell for whatever small sums they were offered.

Members of the ACLU's national committee and board of directors debated the question of whether, in time of war, the government could constitutionally detain citizens as a matter of military necessity. Their decision was that the government did have the right to establish military zones and remove persons from those zones—but that the removals should be determined and carried out by civilian authorities "in a manner, and based upon a classification, having a reasonable relationship to the danger intended to be met." The ACLU thus took the position, as described in one of its reports, that it opposed "removals by military authorities, all mass evacuations, detention after evacuation, and all unreasonable applications of what was conceded to be an underlying constitutional right." And it opposed "the concept of military necessity as applied to so huge an area. . . ."

In the face of nationwide anti-Japanese hysteria and general approval of the removals, ACLU spokesmen publicly deplored them as "the worst single wholesale violation of civil rights of American citizens in our history." ACLU affiliates were urged to bring test cases in protest. One such case, handled by the southern California branch, sought to obtain the freedom of a group of internees by proving their detention unconstitutional. But the internees themselves insisted that the case be dropped. If it should be won, they said, and they and their fellow-internees were released, they would have no place to go because they had all lost their homes. Another case sought freedom for a man who had evaded military authorities and reached Wisconsin. That case was lost, and the man was interned.

When the government eventually adopted a policy of releasing those Japanese aliens and Japanese-American citizens found to be loyal to the United States, the ACLU helped the agencies attempting to provide them with homes and jobs. After the war it lobbied successfully to obtain compensation from Congress for property taken from the internees, and backed further efforts to compensate them for their time of internment.

The fact remained, however, that during the war the inmates of those concentration camps had been deprived of their most basic civil rights. And there are those who still contend that the ACLU's protests against the denial of those rights were much too mild.

In 1879 Connecticut passed a law forbidding the use of contraceptives by anyone within the state's borders, including married couples. It was tested in the U.S. Supreme Court eighty-six years later.

That case, supported by an ACLU friend-of-the-court brief, began in New Haven. There the information center of the Planned Parenthood League of Connecticut was giving birth control advice and instruction to married couples. In November of 1961 the New Haven police ordered the center to suspend all activity. Mrs. Mary Griswold, the league's executive director, and Dr. George Buxton, a Yale

Medical School professor, were found guilty of breaking the 1879 law, and each was fined $100.

When the U.S. Supreme Court finally heard the case, four years later, the majority decision was that the ancient law was unconstitutional.

As Justice William O. Douglas put it, "We deal with a right of privacy older than the Bill of Rights—older than our political parties, older than our school system."

Griswold v. *Connecticut,* as the case was called, gave constitutional protection to marital privacy.

In 1958 Richard Loving, a white man, married a part-Indian, part-black woman in Washington, D.C., and they moved to Virginia. There, several weeks later, they were arrested and accused of evading a Virginia law barring interracial marriages. (Sixteen other states had similar laws at that time.) The Lovings were sentenced to a year in prison, but their sentence was suspended when the couple agreed to leave Virginia immediately and "not return together or at the same time . . . for 25 years."

After five years in Washington, the Lovings decided to fight the law that had banished them from Virginia. With the support of the National Capital Area CLU, their case was taken to a federal district court from which, in due time, it reached the U.S. Supreme Court.

Chief Justice Earl Warren delivered that Court's unanimous decision. The question, he wrote, was:

whether a statutory scheme adopted by the State of Virginia to prevent marriages between persons solely on the basis of racial classification violates the Equal Protection and Due Process Clauses of the Fourteenth Amendment. For reasons which seem to us to reflect the central meaning of those constitutional commands, we conclude that these statutes cannot stand consistently with the Fourteenth Amendment.

A statute that "cannot stand" must obviously fall. The Virginia law was, as lawyers say, knocked down by the unanimous decision. Mr. and Mrs. Richard Loving could live in Virginia without fear of arrest. And the question of the constitutionality of interracial marriage laws was settled.

Or was it?

In the spring of 1980, when the authors were in the small Montgomery office of the Alabama Civil Liberties Union collecting material for this book, a phone call came in. The director of the Montgomery office listened for several minutes, asked some questions, and ended the conversation with: "You'd better come in and give us the details."

Then she put down the phone and turned to us. "That was a black man," she said. "He's just been refused a marriage license because the woman he plans to marry is white."

We stared at her. "But the Supreme Court knocked down interracial marriage laws in 1967!" one of us said. "Alabama officials can't deny a marriage license on those grounds."

"They just did," she said. "We may have to fight that battle all over again."

And suddenly some words of Roger Baldwin's, often quoted in our hearing, came vividly alive to us: "No fight for civil liberties ever stays won."

Perhaps some of the cases described in the following chapters will seem trivial compared to those already mentioned. The ACLU doesn't think they are. It believes that a threat to any civil right, if not recognized and challenged, becomes a threat to all the civil rights guaranteed to all of us by the Constitution.

2

Due Process: A Major Right for Minors

Early in the morning, on June 8, 1964, the telephone rang in a house in the small copper-mining town of Globe, Arizona. A woman picked up the receiver and said hello. When a boy's voice asked if she was Mrs. Cook, the woman said she was. The voice then said that someone wanted to speak to her, and an instant later another boy's voice came over the wire. This one uttered a series of remarks and questions that were, as a judge said later, "of the irritatingly offensive, adolescent, sex variety."

Mrs. Cook hung up abruptly and then called the police to complain. She believed she could identify the caller who had spoken the offensive words as a teen-ager named Ronald Lewis, who lived with his father in a trailer court outside the city limits. Mrs. Cook, who did housework, sometimes cleaned the Lewis trailer.

Since the trailer court was not under the jurisdiction of the Globe police, Mrs. Cook's complaint was referred to the county sheriff's office. About ten o'clock a deputy sheriff pulled into the trailer court looking for Ronald Lewis. The deputy found him and his friend Gerald Gault in the trailer occupied by the Gault family.

The two boys were alone. Gerald's older brother, Louis, a miner, was at work. Paul Gault, the father, was at his job in a gas station up near the Grand Canyon. Marjorie Gault, the mother, cleaned houses to augment the meager family income and was also at work when the deputy sheriff arrived.

The deputy questioned the two boys, learned that they had indeed made the phone call, and took them both to the Children's Detention Home. Apparently he made no effort to find and notify either Mr. or Mrs. Gault or Mr. Lewis, Ronald's only parent, of the arrest of their children. No notice of the arrest was left at either trailer.

When Mrs. Gault came home about six o'clock that evening and discovered Gerald missing, she sent Louis to look for him. He soon discovered what had happened to the two boys. Mrs. Gault was understandably distressed. And her anxiety was heightened by the fact that fifteen-year-old Gerald was still subject to a six-month probation order, the result of having been found in the company of another boy who had stolen money from a woman's purse.

Mrs. Gault and her older son immediately went to the detention home. A probation officer there told them that

Gerald was being held primarily as a witness to the obscene remarks made by Ronald, and that a hearing would take place in juvenile court the next afternoon. This verbal communication was Mrs. Gault's only notice of the impending hearing.

Ronald Lewis was not involved in the subsequent legal procedure because his father had told the court that he had already made plans to leave Arizona to look for work elsewhere. Charges against Ronald were dropped so that he could accompany his father.

On June 9, before the hearing started, the probation officer filed a petition about Gerald with the juvenile court. It stated, without presenting any facts to back up the assertion, that the "said minor is a delinquent minor," and requested a court order for the "care and custody of said minor." Gerald's mother was not given a copy of the petition. Neither she nor her husband saw it until two months later, at a subsequent court session.

Present at the hearing in the chambers of the juvenile court were Judge Robert McGhee, two probation officers, Gerald, his mother, and his brother, Louis. Precisely what was said at the hearing has never been determined, because Judge McGhee decided that the formality of making a transcript, or recording, of the proceedings was unnecessary. He also dispensed with the formality of swearing in any witnesses.

It was Mrs. Gault's later recollection that Gerald had persisted in claiming that he had done nothing more than dial Mrs. Cook's number for Ronald. The probation officers and the judge said just as firmly that Gerald had admitted making some of the lewd statements. Judge McGhee did say that the statements Gerald had admitted making were the less lewd ones, but that didn't alter the situation. Gerald's status had somehow been changed from a witness to a defendant. And, to add to Mrs. Gault's worry, Judge McGhee told her that because Gerald was on probation he could be committed to an institution if he were found guilty of the present charge. Then he adjourned the hearing, saying that he would have to think further about the case before coming to a decision.

The judge sent Gerald back to the detention home to await that decision, instead of sending him home with his mother. He offered no explanation for this action. Nor is there any explanation in any of the documents compiled afterward for Gerald's sudden release. That took place on June 11, according to the probation officer, or on June 12, according to Mrs. Gault.

About five o'clock on the day of Gerald's release, Mrs. Gault received a note from the probation officer stating that another hearing had been scheduled for the morning of June 15. That note, on plain paper, bearing no designation of the court, was the only notice of the second hearing that Mrs. Gault received.

This time both parents appeared with Gerald. Again, as at the previous hearing, no record was made of the proceedings. Evidently, Gerald again denied having made any obscene remarks, and the judge persisted in claiming that he had earlier admitted having made some. The Gaults and the judge did later agree, however, that during the hearing Mrs. Gault had asked why the complainant, Mrs. Cook, was not there, so she could see which boy "had done the dirty talking over the phone." And they agreed on the judge's response: that Mrs. Cook didn't have to be present at the hearing because the probation officer had talked to her over the phone. The judge himself never communicated with Mrs. Cook to discover what she had to say.

During this June 15 hearing, a report written by Gerald's probation officer was submitted to the judge. It was not shown to Gerald's parents, so they had no opportunity to rebut any charges in it.

The judge announced his decision when he ended the hearing. He declared Gerald a juvenile delinquent and committed him to the Arizona State Industrial School "for the period of his minority, unless sooner discharged by due process of law." The official order said that the decision was reached "after a full hearing and due deliberation."

Gerald had been given a sentence that could keep him under confinement for six years, until he was twenty-one. An adult convicted of making an obscene phone call could not have been fined more than $50 and sent to jail for more than two months.

Gerald's case was not unique. Since the reformation of juvenile justice early in the century, juveniles were being judged and sentenced in courts as informal as Judge McGhee's. But by 1964 there was a good deal of opposition to that informality, which could so easily lead to decisions based on a judge's whim. The belief had been growing that juvenile offenders were often treated unfairly, that sentences were often arbitrary and far out of line with offenses, that young people's rights were being trampled on.

The Gaults probably were not concerned with the general practice of juvenile justice in the United States. But they certainly were concerned about the way their son had been treated in Judge McGhee's court. They believed Gerald when he denied making the obscene remarks to Mrs. Cook. They believed his claim that he had just put the call through for Ronald from the trailer court's public pay phone. The Gaults thought Mrs. Cook should have been required to testify and identify the voice that had uttered the obscene words.

Gerald's parents decided to do what they could to get Judge McGhee's decision changed. They managed to scrape together $180, and Mr. Gault went looking for a lawyer to take their case. He was turned down by one lawyer who said he couldn't handle the case because he was a friend of the judge. Two other attorneys refused the case because they were connected in some way with city or county government.

Paul Gault then went to the office of the district attorney, seeking advice as to where he could obtain legal help. There he talked to Philip Haggerty, an assistant attorney, who refused to hear any details of the case because he might, he said, find himself on the other side of the legal action. But Haggerty did recommend another lawyer. She was Amelia D. Lewis, who had recently moved to Sun City, Arizona, from New York, where she had practiced law for some time and been associated with the ACLU. Haggerty called Lewis while Gault was still in his office and told her of Gault's problem. She agreed to come to Globe—some ninety miles east of Sun City—to interview the Gaults.

As a new lawyer in Arizona, Amelia Lewis was pleased to have a client. She was even more pleased to fight for a client who had, in her opinion, been deprived of some of the basic rights guaranteed by the Constitution. The fact that Gerald Gault was a minor should not, she believed, have put him beyond the protection of the due process of the law. And from the statements given to her by Mr. and Mrs. Gault, there was no doubt in her mind that Gerald had not been protected.

But while she relished the prospect of taking on the Arizona juvenile court system, she knew, through her association with the ACLU, that such a fight could be a long one and cost considerably more money than the Gaults were likely to have. So she explained to Gerald's parents that, while she would be glad to take Gerald's case and the money they had scraped together would be enough to start the proceedings, the case might have to be appealed to higher courts—possibly even to the Supreme Court of the United States. Money for such appeals, she explained, probably would be available from sources interested in constitutional rights. But, she asked the Gaults, were they willing to spend the time and effort to see the case through to its end?

The Gaults, upset and angry about Gerald's treatment, told her they were. They put it in writing on the statements they had already given her, which she notarized. Then Amelia Lewis started the legal moves necessary to carry Gerald's case to a higher Arizona court.

What Lewis wanted to win for Gerald—and for all young people—was, in essence, the protection offered by the Fourteenth Amendment to the Constitution, which states ". . . nor shall any State deprive any person of life, liberty, or property, without the due process of the law." And due process includes the right to confront one's accuser, the right to have a lawyer, the right to timely notification of the charges, the right to examine and cross-examine witnesses under oath, the right to a record of the trial proceedings, and the right to be notified of the privilege of remaining silent.

When Lewis went to file an appeal from Judge Mc-Ghee's ruling, she discovered that Arizona law did not allow appeals from juvenile courts. So she applied, instead, for a writ of *habeas corpus* to the Supreme Court of Arizona. (Those Latin words mean, literally, you shall have the body, and a writ of *habeas corpus* is issued by a court to secure the release of a person from unlawful confinement.)

The Arizona Supreme Court told Lewis that she must

first apply to a lower state court. So she carried her petition for a writ of *habeas corpus* to the Superior Court of Arizona. That court, after a hearing, decided that the Globe juvenile court's proceedings were in accordance with Arizona laws and denied the petition. Lewis prepared to take the petition back to the Arizona Supreme Court.

This move involved the printing of all the records of the proceedings that had taken place in the Superior Court—at the cost of some $200. So Lewis went to the Arizona Civil Liberties Union for help. By emptying its meager treasury of all but a few dollars, the ACLU affiliate paid for the necessary printing, and Lewis duly applied to the Arizona Supreme Court for a writ of *habeas corpus*. On December 14, 1965, that court upheld the lower court and refused to issue the writ.

It was now about a year and a half since Gerald had been sentenced. It was, moreover, a year since he had been released from the Arizona State Industrial Home, on probation, after having served six months. But, in Amelia Lewis's opinion, Gerald's release didn't alter the fact that he had been tried and sentenced illegally, and that other young people could be facing the same kind of treatment.

So Lewis called the national office of the ACLU and gave Melvin L. Wulf, the union's legal director, a summary of the case. Would it be possible, she asked, to carry the fight to the federal courts? And, if so, could the union provide the financial help that would be needed to print the Arizona Supreme Court proceedings and do whatever else had to be done before the case could be tried there? Wulf asked Lewis to send him more details. She did. Three days later he called her to say that the ACLU would attempt to take the case to the United States Supreme Court, and that there would be money available for the necessary legal expenses.

When the Supreme Court agreed to hear the case, known as *In Re Gault* (meaning in the matter of Gault), something of a stir swept through legal and judicial circles. Because the Supreme Court agrees to adjudicate only a small fraction of the several thousand cases brought to its attention each year, its decision to rule in the Gault case gave the litigation unusual importance. Furthermore, this was the first time that the highest court in the land had been asked to review a state juvenile court case. If the decision went against Arizona, it would indicate that most juvenile court proceedings were unconstitutional insofar as they deprived young people of the protection of the due process clause.

And that's just what happened.

On May 15, 1967, in a decision written by Justice Abe Fortas, the Supreme Court declared that juvenile courts must grant to children many of the procedural protections guaranteed by the Bill of Rights. As one news magazine put it, the Court showed "undisguised dismay over the state of juvenile justice in most of the U.S."

"Neither the Fourteenth Amendment nor the Bill of Rights," Justice Fortas wrote, "is for adults only. Under our Constitution, the condition of being a boy does not justify a kangaroo court." Since a kangaroo court is generally defined as a mock court, illegally passing and executing judgment, Justice Fortas was voicing a harsh opinion of the juvenile court system.

And Justice Fortas had more to say about the American juvenile justice system. About one-fifth of the judges sitting in the country's 3,000 juvenile courts, he had discovered, were not members of the bar, half of them had no undergraduate college degree, and one-fifth had no college education at all.

"The highest motives and most enlightened impulses led

to the system," Justice Fortas wrote. "But in practice, juvenile court history has again demonstrated that unbridled discretion, however benevolently motivated, is frequently a poor substitute for principle and procedure."

Justice Fortas laid down a few rules for the future practice of juvenile justice. Juveniles, he wrote, must have timely notice of the charges against them; they have the right to a lawyer, appointed by the court if necessary, whenever incarceration is a possible punishment; they have the right to confront and cross-examine complainants and other witnesses; they must be given adequate warning of their privilege against self-incrimination and their right to remain silent.

The vote on the Gault case was eight to one. The lone dissenter feared that the decision might lead to a return to the nineteenth-century judicial practice by which children were tried in regular criminal courts.

But the majority decision had anticipated such an objection by stating that juvenile courts did not have to change completely. Juvenile records, the decision said, still could be kept secret; a young offender still could be classified as a delinquent and not as a criminal; and "nothing will require that the conception of the kindly juvenile judge be replaced by its opposite."

The decision, of course, meant that Gerald's sentence had been declared null and void. It now had no legal standing—it had been erased.

What had started out as a humdrum juvenile hearing and a routine juvenile court disposition of an alleged misdemeanor had turned into a landmark case in the field of juvenile justice. *In Re Gault* is generally considered one of the foundation stones of modern juvenile court procedure.

3

Free Speech in School

The First Amendment to the Constitution of the United States includes these words: "Congress shall make no law . . . abridging the freedom of speech. . . ." The Fourteenth Amendment broadens that prohibition to include the states and their institutions.

Question: Does this constitutional protection of the right of free speech apply to public school students?

Answer: Before February 24, 1969, it rarely did. Since that date it does, with some exceptions.

It was on that date that the United States Supreme Court issued its decision in the case of *Tinker et al.* v. *Des Moines Independent Community School District et al.* (The Latin phrase *et al.,* meaning and others, indicates that other people are also involved.) On the Tinker side there were John F. Tinker, age fifteen; Mary Beth Tinker, age thirteen; and Christopher Eckhardt, age fifteen. On the other side were a number of school and board of education officials of the community school district. It is understandable that in referring to this case—and it is often referred to—it is called simply the Tinker case.

The Tinker and Eckhardt families lived in Des Moines, Iowa, and their children attended elementary and secondary schools in the Des Moines school district. Both families and a number of their friends were among the many Americans who were then opposed to the United States involvement in the Vietnam War. Protests against this involvement had taken many forms: marches, picketing, college campus mass meetings, draft-card burnings. Some of these activities had resulted in arrests and injuries.

The Tinkers, the Eckhardts, and their friends were nonviolent protestors. At a meeting in December 1965, at the Eckhardt house, they decided to make known their feelings about the war by wearing black armbands from December 16 until New Year's Day, and to fast on the first and last day of that "mourning" period. The Tinker children and Christopher Eckhardt were going to join in that silent protest.

At about this time a student in one of the Des Moines high schools told his journalism teacher that he wanted to write an article for the school paper about Vietnam. The teacher reported this request to his supervisors, with the result that on December 14 a meeting of school principals was called to discuss the matter. The principals and other administrators decided they didn't want a controversial article in the school paper, and one principal and the director of secondary education were delegated to tell the student so. They succeeded in dissuading the student but, as they reported later, "we did not feel that we had convinced the student that our decision was a just one."

At the above meeting of principals, a discussion took place about the rumor that some students intended to wear black armbands in school beginning December 16. The principals voted to ban the wearing of armbands on school property and issued a regulation to that effect.

On December 16 John Tinker turned up at North High School wearing his armband. Mary Beth Tinker arrived at Warren Harding Junior High wearing hers. And Christopher Eckhardt wore his to the Roosevelt High School. (Paul Tinker, age eight, and Hope Tinker, age eleven, wore armbands to their elementary schools, but they were not part of the subsequent legal action.)

Each armband-wearing student was told to remove the band. When they refused, they were sent home with instructions not to return to school until they were willing to appear without the black symbol. None of them returned until their self-imposed period of "mourning" was ended, following the holiday vacation.

To the Tinkers and the Eckhardts the suspension of their children for wearing black armbands was a violation of the right of free speech. The Iowa Civil Liberties Union agreed and filed a petition in the United States District Court on the children's behalf, asking for an injunction to stop the school officials from disciplining the petitioners. Since the petitioners were minors, the two fathers acted for their children.

The first question the court had to decide was whether the wearing of a symbol—an armband—was a form of speech protected by the First Amendment. The court decided it was, because of the 1943 Supreme Court decision in *West Virginia* v. *Barnette,* when the Court ruled that Jehovah's Witnesses' children did not have to recite the pledge of allegiance to the flag. Their refusal to do so, the Supreme Court had then said, was a symbolic way of expressing their belief. And the Court had made it clear that the First Amendment protects symbolic expressions as well as spoken ones.

Having decided that the Des Moines petitioners had indeed been deprived of the right of free expression, the district court faced the question of the school officials' right to deprive them of it. And here, too, there were legal precedents to use as guides. But there was also the traditional reluctance of a court to intervene in school affairs. Educators, courts have generally held, know more about education than judges do. Furthermore, courts have acted in the belief that school officials have the responsibilities and duties of parents while children are in school, and may discipline their charges in order to maintain an atmosphere in which learning can take place. So, historically, judges have not as a rule vigorously defended the civil rights of students in school disciplinary cases.

The Tinker case is a good example of the conflict—still not fully resolved today—between the duty of school officials to maintain order and the right of students to the protection of the Constitution. The district court resolved the conflict in the Tinker case by supporting the school officials in a decision announced on September 1, 1966.

"The avowed purpose of the plaintiffs in this instance was to express their views on a controversial subject by wearing black armbands in the schools," the district court stated.

While the armbands themselves may not be disruptive, the reactions and comments from other students as a result of the
armbands would be likely to disturb the disciplined atmosphere required for any classroom. . . . The school officials
involved had a reasonable basis for adopting the armband regulation.

On the other hand the plaintiffs' freedom of speech is in-
fringed upon only to a limited extent. They are still free to wear
armbands off school premises. . . . It is vitally important that
the interest of students . . . in current affairs be encouraged
whenever possible. In this instance, however, it is the disciplined atmosphere of the classroom, not the plaintiffs' right to
wear armbands on school premises, which is entitled to the
protection of the law.

The Iowa Civil Liberties Union, unwilling to accept that
decision, took the case to the United States Court of Appeals in the Eighth Circuit. The eight judges of that court,
after reading the briefs of both sides and listening to oral
arguments, were evenly divided. Four were in favor of upholding the district court's decision; four were in favor of
reversing it and upholding the students' right to wear black
armbands. That even division meant that the district court
decision would automatically be allowed to stand.

The Civil Liberties Union then petitioned the Supreme
Court of the United States to hear the Tinker case. The
Supreme Court agreed, and the case was argued November 12, 1968. The decision was announced February 24,
1969, a little more than four years after the Tinkers and
Christopher Eckhardt had been suspended from their
schools. By a vote of seven to two, the Supreme Court
reversed the district court decision and ruled that the Des
Moines school officials had denied the petitioners their

rights under the First Amendment.

The Tinker decision has become a landmark in the field of juvenile civil rights. Quotations from the majority decision, written by Justice Abe Fortas, have peppered the briefs of civil rights lawyers ever since.

"It can hardly be argued," Justice Fortas wrote, "that either students or teachers shed their constitutional rights to freedom of speech or expression at the schoolhouse gates." But he also appreciated the right of school officials to use disciplinary measures to maintain order. He wrote that "the Court has repeatedly emphasized the need for affirming the comprehensive authority of the States and of school authorities, consistent with fundamental constitutional safeguards, to prescribe and control conduct in the schools."

But the Tinker case, he said, should not be compared to such ordinary school disciplinary problems as those involving dress, hair length, or aggressive and disruptive student behavior. The Tinker case directly involved First Amendment rights.

"The school officials banned and sought to punish petitioners for a silent, passive expression of opinion, unaccompanied by any disorder or disturbance on the part of the petitioners," Justice Fortas wrote.

There is here no evidence whatever of the petitioners' interference, actual or nascent, with the school's work, or of collision with the rights of other students to be let alone. . . .

The District Court concluded that the action of the school authorities was reasonable because it was based on their fear of a disturbance from the wearing of armbands. . . . Any departure from absolute regimentation may cause trouble. Any variation from the majority's opinion may inspire fear. Any word spoken in class, in the lunchroom or on the campus, that deviates from the view of another person, may start an argument or cause a disturbance. But our Constitution says we must take this risk . . . and our history says it is this sort of hazardous freedom—this kind of openness—that is the basis of our National strength and of the independence and vigor of Americans who grow up and live in this relatively permissive, often disputatious society.

Replying to the district court's contention that controversial issues should be aired in orderly classroom discussions, the decision stated that

Freedom of expression could not truly exist if the right could be exercised only in an area that a benevolent government has provided as a safe haven for crackpots. The constitution says that Congress (and the States) may not abridge the right to free speech. This provision means what it says. We properly read it to permit reasonable regulation of speech-connected activities in carefully restricted circumstances. But we do not confine the permissible exercise of First Amendment rights to a telephone booth or to the four corners of a pamphlet, or to supervised and ordained discussion in a school classroom.

With these words the Supreme Court laid down the precept that, with "reasonable regulations," a student's right of free speech was protected not only during classroom discussions but at any time in the school or on its grounds. Because the decision also put forth the idea that "Students in school as well as out of school are 'persons' under our Constitution," it is easy to understand why the Tinker case has assumed such importance.

The vigorous dissent to that opinion, however, written by Justice Hugo Black, is also frequently cited by lawyers and judges. Justice Black, who had built a reputation as one of the Court's strongest defenders of the Bill of Rights, was staunch in his defense of the right of educators to run their institutions without undue hindrance from the courts. To Justice Black the crucial questions in the case were

whether students and teachers may use the schools at their whim as a platform for the exercise of free speech—"symbolic" or "pure"—and whether the courts will allocate to themselves the function of deciding how the pupils' school day will be spent. While I have always believed that under the First and Fourteenth Amendments neither the State nor the Federal Government has any authority to regulate or censor the content of a speech, I have never believed that any person has a right to give speeches or engage in demonstrations where he pleases and when he pleases.

Justice Black went on to say:

Here a very small number of students had crisply and summarily refused to obey a school order designed to give pupils who want to learn the opportunity to do so. One does not need to be a prophet or the son of a prophet to know that after the Court's holding today some students in Iowa schools and indeed in all schools will be ready, able, and willing to defy their teachers on practically all orders. . . . I, for one, am not fully persuaded that school pupils are wise enough, even with this Court's expert help from Washington, to run the 23,390 public school systems in our 50 States.

Predictably, the reaction of the press was varied. David Lawrence, writing in the March 10, 1969, issue of *U.S. News*, was even more vehement than Justice Black in his denunciation of the majority verdict. "How, in the face of the High Court's new decision," Lawrence asked, "can the schools effectively teach patriotism and a love of country?"

The Washington *Evening Star* saw other dangers in the decision. "No particular expertise is required to see how wide a door has been opened. Any minute now some mini-skirted teenie-bopper or long-haired adolescent will come up with a high-minded cause for which they must speak up—symbolically—by displaying their thighs or hiding their ears."

The *New York Times*, on the other hand, pointed out that the decision did not rule out restrictions on free speech in the schools. "There is no license given here to riot, to interfere with classroom work," it said editorially.

The one aspect of the Tinker case about which there seems to be little disagreement is that it gave rise to one of the most important Supreme Court decisions ever issued on the civil rights of minors.

4

Arbitrary Suspensions Nullified

Is a suspended public school student deprived of liberty or property by being kept out of school? And, if so, is the student protected by the Fourteenth Amendment, which says that no state may deprive any person of "life, liberty, or property without due process of law"?

These questions were taken all the way to the United States Supreme Court for answers. And in January 1975, that court ruled that suspending a student *was* a deprivation of liberty and property, and that students *were* protected, to some extent, by the Fourteenth Amendment's due process clause.

The legal case that led to that decision—it is usually referred to as *Goss* v. *Lopez*—started in a U.S. district court in Ohio. It represented the efforts of nine suspended public school students to win for themselves, and for all students in similar situations, the benefits of legal due process. The defendant against whom they brought their lawsuit was the Columbus, Ohio, school system.

The American Civil Liberties Union, although not directly representing the students, did file an *amicus curiae* brief supporting them, as did several other organizations. An *amicus* brief supporting the Columbus school system was filed by the Buckeye Association of School Administrators.

The nine suspensions had all occurred during a period of considerable turmoil in and around several Columbus schools in February and March of 1971. The turmoil arose because black students' requests to have black community leaders address school assemblies during a black history week had been refused by the school administrators. The students staged demonstrations to protest the refusal. Some were orderly, some were not. Among the students suspended for disorderly conduct were those who later decided to sue the school system.

Dwight Lopez, in whose name *Goss* v. *Lopez* was started, was a student at Central High School. (Norval Goss was the school administrator in whose name the case was appealed to the Supreme Court.) According to his testimony in court, Lopez was in the lunchroom on the morning of February 26, 1971, when a group of students entered and began overturning the tables. Lopez and several others left the room to avoid trouble, and shortly afterward, when the school was ordered closed for the day, Lopez went home.

That same afternoon he received a phone call from the principal, telling him that he had been suspended.

Others of the nine were suspended from their own schools for different reasons. At Marion-Franklin High School, for example, a police officer had been called to remove the leader of a group of students who had entered the auditorium while a class was in session there and had refused an order to leave. The student leader was immediately suspended. So was another student who thereupon attacked the officer. A third Marion-Franklin High School student was suspended because she allegedly had left her study group and "gone into the halls and created a disturbance."

A thirteen-year-old McGuffey Junior High School girl was also among the nine. According to her court testimony, her first-period class had been dismissed because of a disturbance in the hall, and she and other students had gone out into the playground. They had remained there until the principal told them to go home. On her way the thirteen-year-old had passed Linden McKinley High School, where a disturbance was taking place. She had been picked up by the police officers called in to control it and taken to the juvenile bureau. Her mother, called by the police, had soon arrived and taken her daughter home. No charges were filed against the girl. But the next morning her mother was notified that the girl had been suspended by the principal of her own school.

The nine students were suspended for periods varying from several days to more than ten. Some were allowed to return afterward to their own schools; others were transferred. Several shifted to night schools of their own accord. By the time the suit against the school officials was finally heard by the three-man district court in 1973, all who were juniors or seniors at the time of suspension had been graduated from one school or another.

Despite the variety in the individual cases, all had one thing in common. Each suspension had been ordered without the student having been given a hearing, either before the suspension or within a reasonable time afterward. No student had had the opportunity to offer a defense or to claim mitigating circumstances for the alleged misdeeds or rule violations. None, in other words, had enjoyed the protection guaranteed by the Fourteenth Amendment.

The students and the organizations supporting them set three goals that they hoped the court hearing would achieve. One was to establish that the students had indeed been deprived of property and liberty without due process of law, and that therefore the Columbus Board of Education's rules regarding suspension were unconstitutional. Another was to insure the removal of all suspension records from the students' files. The third was to have the lawsuit declared a class action, meaning that the nine students represented all Columbus public school students who had been suspended during that troubled period or who might face suspension in the future.

The Columbus education officials did not admit the legal basis for any of the student claims. One of their lines of defense was to point out that nothing in the Constitution guarantees the right to an education at public expense. Therefore, the officials argued, public school students could not claim that the Constitution protected them from being temporarily deprived of something they had no constitutional right to possess.

The school officials also claimed the long-recognized right of teachers to maintain order in the schools by disciplining their students. And they produced the scholastic records of the nine students to show that the suspensions had had little or no effect on their grade averages.

The students' lawyers countered with the claim that suspensions are a serious form of punishment that can cause psychological harm, loss of self-esteem, a feeling of resentment against teachers, and a sense of helplessness and inadequacy. Suspension, the lawyers contended, could brand a student as a troublemaker, a person to be viewed with suspicion. It could lead to a student's withdrawal from participation in school activities and eventual academic failure.

The district court recognized that the educators had, as they claimed, followed the rules of their system, and that those rules did not provide for due process in suspension cases. The court also agreed with the Columbus school system's contention that there was no such thing as a constitutional right to a free education.

But, said the court, the state of Ohio had created a free school system and had made education compulsory for all between the ages of six and eighteen. Furthermore, the court said, education had become a virtual necessity for successful life in a democratic society. Therefore, the court ruled, education was, in effect, a valuable property created by the state and one that the state could not take away, even temporarily, without due process of law.

As to whether a suspension deprived a student of liberty, the district court quoted from a 1972 decision by the United States Supreme Court. The concept of liberty, that decision said, included "not merely freedom from bodily restraint, but also the right . . . to engage in any of the common occupations of life, to acquire useful knowledge."

So, the district court summed up, the Columbus school system had deprived students of both property and liberty without the due process of law and had, therefore, acted unconstitutionally. The court ruled, in addition, that the lawsuit could be declared a class action affecting "all students of the Columbus Public Schools suspended on or after February, 1971." And the court ordered that references to suspensions imposed unconstitutionally during that month's turmoil be removed from all student records.

No hard and fast rules of disciplinary procedures were laid down by the court, because it believed the school officials were better qualified than judges to make such rules. But it did interpret what it called "the minimum procedural process mandated by the Constitution" for suspensions of ten days or less. According to the court's interpretation, school officials were required to:

Give the student and the student's parents, within 24 hours after a suspension, a written notice stating the terms of the suspension and the reasons for it.

Give the student and the student's parents, not later than 72 hours after the actual removal of the student from school, the opportunity to attend a hearing before a school administrator. The hearing would not be a judicial proceeding—no counsel would be required for the student—but it must provide statements supporting the charges against the student, and a chance for the student and others to present statements explaining or defending the alleged misconduct.

Advise the student and the student's parents by letter, within 24 hours after that hearing, of the school officials' decision and their reasons for it.

The Columbus public school system immediately appealed the district court's decision to the United States Supreme Court. Lawyers for both sides argued before the Supreme Court on October 16, 1974. The justices handed down their decision on January 22, 1975. By a narrow majority they upheld the district court. Justice Byron R. White wrote the opinion agreed to by five of the nine justices.

Justice Lewis E. Powell wrote the opinion expressing the vigorous dissent of the remaining four. Both opinions would be widely and frequently cited in the future. Justice White wrote:

The student's interest is to avoid unfair or mistaken exclusion from the educational process, with all of its unfortunate consequences. The Due Process Clause will not shield him from suspension properly imposed, but it disserves both his interest and the interest of the State if his suspension is in fact unwarranted. The concern would be mostly academic if the disciplinary process were a totally accurate, unerring process, never mistaken and never unfair. Unfortunately this is not the case, and no one suggests that it is. . . . The risk of error is not at all trivial, and it should be guarded against if that may be done without prohibitive cost or interference with the educational process. . . .

Justice Powell, who had once served on a Virginia board of education, argued that the majority opinion "unnecessarily opens avenues for judicial intervention in the operation of our public schools that may seriously affect the quality of education." It justified that "unprecedented intrusion," he said, "by identifying a new constitutional right: the right of a student not to be suspended for as much as a single day without notice and a due process hearing either before or promptly following the suspension." He went on:

The Court ignores the experience of mankind as well as the long history of our law recognizing that there *are* differences which must be accommodated in determining the rights and duties of children as compared with those of adults. . . . Until today, and except in the special context of the first Amendment issue in *Tinker,* the educational rights of children and teenagers in the elementary and secondary school have not been analogized to the rights of adults or to those accorded college students.

Justice Powell had not been convinced by the argument that a student could be psychologically damaged by a brief suspension. And he amplified that theme in a footnote:

There is no doubt a school of modern psychological or psychiatric persuasion that maintains that *any* discipline of the young is detrimental. . . . In my view we tend to lose our sense of perspective and proportion in a case of this kind. For average, normal children—the vast majority—suspension for a few days is simply *not* a detriment; it is a commonplace occurrence, with some 10% of all students being suspended; it leaves no scars; affects no reputations; indeed it may often be viewed by the young as a badge of some distinction and a welcome holiday.

Justice Powell was expressing the views of those who believe that what public education needs is more discipline, not less. Justice White and the majority of the Court were expressing—to some extent, at least—the views of those who believe that young students are "persons" under the Constitution and thus deserve the protection of the Bill of Rights.

How much of the Bill of Rights is applicable to juveniles is still being argued. But *Goss* v. *Lopez,* which required school officials to provide at least the "minimum" constitutional protection for students threatened with suspension, did reinforce the idea that the right to due process of law is not reserved for adults only.

5

The Case of M.M.

DEAN FORCES HS GIRL TO STRIP IN DRUG SEARCH

A 15-year-old girl suspected of carrying marijuana was forced by a Bayside HS dean to undergo a strip search, the *Post* has learned.

The search turned up nothing. . . .

The American Civil Liberties Union is considering legal action on behalf of the student. . . .

—The *New York Post,* Monday, March 6, 1978

A number of readers must have been puzzled by the prominence the *Post* gave that story. A typical New Yorker's response might well have been, "So—what else is new?" Stories about drug users and drug pushers among high school students were not unusual in 1978. Nor were reports of student searches or student possession of stolen property and weapons, which had resulted in arrests by the police. Why, then, should the search of one girl—even a strip search—be worth that much space in the *Post*? And why should the American Civil Liberties Union consider spending time and money on the case?

John L. Mitchell was the *Post* reporter who had written the story after talking to Richard Emery, a legal counsel of the New York Civil Liberties Union, the ACLU's New York affiliate. Mitchell hadn't learned about the search until four months after it took place. If he hadn't learned of it at all, an important case in the history of the struggle for students' civil rights might never have reached the courtroom.

Mitchell first found out about the search late in February 1978, when he was seeking material for another story in the board of education's Office of School Security. An employee of that office, aware of Mitchell's reputation as an investigative reporter, showed him an account that he said might be the basis of a "hell of a story." It was a description of the strip search at Bayside High School, written by Christine Gilbert, the security guard who had been called in to witness it.

Gilbert, as part of her regular duties, witnessed dozens of searches a year. Normally they followed the guidelines issued by the New York City Board of Education: If any school principal, dean, or teacher had a reasonable suspicion that a student possessed anything illegal—drugs, weapons, or stolen property—that student's book bag or purse might be searched and the student might be "patted down," or frisked.

But on October 27, 1977, for the first time, Gilbert had seen a student stripped nearly naked during a search—a procedure she had never even heard of. And because fellow security guards suggested to her that she might have witnessed an unlawful act, she had written an account of it for her supervisor, omitting the names of both the woman dean and the student involved. She had added to her account a brief description of another search for drugs made by the same dean shortly afterward, which Gilbert also witnessed. In that case a student openly in possession of drug paraphernalia had been asked merely to "zip down her boots and back up again." Although Gilbert's report did not state that the first girl was black and the second girl was white, it implied the question: Why had the two girls been treated so differently?

Christine Gilbert and her supervisor, who had handed the account on to his superiors, had both assumed that an investigation would be made of what had happened on October 27 at Bayside High School. But no investigation had taken place. Instead, Mitchell learned, Gilbert had been summarily transferred to another school for having "violated the confidentiality of Bayside." And her supervisor had been reprimanded by his chief in a letter that said, "The principal is in charge of his school. He sets policy and apparently he has authorized its staff to make searches of students when deemed necessary."

Mitchell left the school security office that February day with what he thought might be the nucleus of an important story for readers of the *Post*. He almost changed his mind after interviewing the principal of Bayside, a school of some 4,000 students in New York's crowded borough of Queens. The principal was proud that among the city's hundreds of schools, his was considered a "good" one, with a higher academic rating than that of many others. In response to Mitchell's questions, he said he had "thoroughly" investigated the incident Gilbert had reported and that the "allegations that a student was made to strip are false."

But Mitchell continued his queries and reached the conclusion that the substance of Gilbert's account was true. He also decided he could trust himself not to be influenced by one of the facts he had learned: Gilbert, as well as the strip-searched girl, were both, like himself, black; the Bayside principal and the dean, and the girl whose search had been limited to her boots, were all white.

That was when Mitchell made the first of two important phone calls to Emery, the NYCLU lawyer. Was a student constitutionally protected, he asked Emery, against the kind of strip search Christine Gilbert had described?

Emery told him that, in the opinion of the ACLU, the answer to his question was yes: Young people, as well as adults, are entitled to the full protection of the Constitution's Fourth Amendment, which states that people shall be "secure in their persons, houses, papers, and effects, against unreasonable searches and seizures," and that a warrant permitting a legal search shall be issued only upon "probable cause," and "particularly describing the things to be seized."

But, Emery added, searches that would be illegal under a strict interpretation of that amendment did in fact take place in schools and had even been upheld in the courts. The reasoning in such cases was that the special relationship between teachers and students—similar in some ways to that between parents and children—gave a teacher the right to act as a parent might act in certain situations. One of these situations might occur if a teacher decided to search a student. The teacher would not have to claim that it was likely—or probable, to use the word in the

amendment—that the student possessed, say, stolen property. With the good of that one student—and of all the
teacher's other students—in mind, the teacher might conduct the search with only a reasonable suspicion of the
presence of stolen goods.

Emery pointed out that even *The Rights of Students,*
the ACLU's own recently published handbook for students, advised its readers that "Until the courts rule that
the Fourth Amendment unambiguously applies to students in school, you should assume you may be searched."

Still, Emery said, it might be possible to prove in court
that a specific strip search of a fifteen-year-old student had
been illegal. He said he would be interested in knowing
anything further Mitchell learned about the case. Emery
knew and respected the *Post* reporter, and trusted his
judgment.

Mitchell then went to talk to the searched student, Marsha Martin (that's not her real name), and her mother. He
found Mrs. Martin a sober, devoutly Christian woman. She
was a licensed practical hospital nurse and the wife of a
steelworker. Of her six children, Marsha was next to the
youngest, and Mrs. Martin was still clearly upset over what
had happened to her. She said she had felt she couldn't
tell her husband about it because she knew it would make
him very angry, and he sometimes behaved rashly when
his temper was aroused. But she had tried to take some
action herself, and she told Mitchell about that.

Soon after the search had taken place, she said, she had
had a phone call from Christine Gilbert, a woman she had
then only heard of through Marsha and still hadn't met.
Gilbert had said that she was ready to testify about the
search she had witnessed, if Mrs. Martin planned to take
legal action against the school authorities. Encouraged by
that offer, Mrs. Martin had then sought help from a lawyer. But he had advised her that it would be useless to try

to bring such a case against the board of education. And so, Mrs. Martin said, she had given up because she didn't know what else to do.

Mitchell made his second telephone call to Emery from the Martin house. He said he thought Emery might be interested in questioning the Martins himself. Emery asked Mitchell to bring Marsha and her mother to the NYCLU office, if they were willing to talk to him.

The Martins came. Emery looked at Marsha. She was a thin girl, tall for her age, but with a figure that was still undeveloped. She seemed, as Emery later described her, "an outwardly defiant girl, who is really a little insecure." They all sat down together, and Emery asked Marsha to tell him what had happened on the day she was allegedly stripped and searched.

Marsha seemed reluctant to repeat her story to a stranger. But once she started she spoke quickly, as if—Emery thought—she were describing a series of events she was watching at that very moment on a television screen.

The first of those events showed Marsha herself in a poor light. It began with the ringing of the fire-drill bell during her tenth-grade English class. The teacher, Terisa Ragin, had told her students to leave their book bags on their desks and follow her into the corridor and down into the street. All obeyed except Marsha. Marsha knew it was a punishable offense to remain inside the building during a fire drill. But she had stayed behind, she said, so that she could do something else she knew she'd be punished for if she were caught: She wanted to take some of the posters from the room's bulletin board—funny Marx Brothers posters—to decorate her small niece's room.

She had already removed two of the posters when she heard footsteps and the jangling of keys in the corridor. Some faculty member, she realized, must be checking the building to make sure it was empty of students. Marsha crouched behind the room's half-open door, hoping she wouldn't be seen.

A moment later she glanced up into the face of a man peering through the door's glass panel. Edmund Janko, a dean of boys at the school, was looking down at her.

Dean Janko opened the door wider and came in. He asked Marsha for her name and an explanation.

Emery, listening to Marsha's story, thought the dean had suspected her of robbing the book bags that had been left on the deserted classroom desks.

Marsha, hurrying now, told Emery she'd admitted to Dean Janko that she was taking the posters. But she had refused to tell him her name.

"I asked him not to report me," she said. "I didn't want the school to have to tell my mother about it."

Dean Janko had moved toward the front of the room just as Marsha heard the buzz and clatter of hundreds of students in the halls. The fire drill was over. Behind Janko's back she slipped through the door and into the crowd. Then, suddenly aware that she had left her book bag behind, she asked the first friend she saw to go into the room and get it for her.

The friend agreed, but the bag she brought out a few minutes later, though it looked like Marsha's, wasn't hers. Marsha knew she would have to return the bag and find her own, which held the bus pass and money she needed to get home. Hoping that by this time Dean Janko had left, she went back inside.

But Dean Janko was still there, talking to Mrs. Ragin. Both of them looked at Marsha. Then Dean Janko addressed Marsha by name, said he was taking her to the assistant principal's office, and led her out of the room.

In the assistant principal's office, Dean Janko whispered briefly to Lucille Amicone, a dean of girls. Then he left. Dean Amicone turned to Marsha and asked her where her book bag was.

Marsha said she had left it in room 225, the English classroom, and that she ought to go back there for it right away. Dean Amicone said they would go together.

In room 225 Marsha hunted for her book bag while Dean Amicone and Mrs. Ragin talked quietly together. The bag couldn't be found. Anxious now over its possible loss, Marsha said, "Listen, Miss Amicone . . . I have to find my bag." Dean Amicone, who seemed as eager as Marsha herself for the bag to be found, said they would go to the lost-and-found office and see if it had been brought there.

But in the hall, on their way, they met several girls from Marsha's English class. One of them said, "Here, Marsha—here's your bag."

Then, Marsha told Emery, Dean Amicone took her back to the assistant principal's office, through which they passed into a small inner room. There the dean ordered Marsha to empty her bag on the table.

"I said, 'Miss Amicone, even though you don't have a search warrant, I'm going to empty my bag for you, right?' " Marsha told Emery. And she did, turning the bag upside down over the one table in the small room and letting everything in it fall out—books, gloves, pens, purse, and her bus-pass case.

Dean Amicone looked through the books. She examined the gloves and asked Marsha if she had found them.

"I told her my mother bought me the gloves," Marsha said indignantly to Emery. Then, while Dean Amicone "felt" her coat, Marsha began to return her belongings to her book bag. When Dean Amicone saw her pick up her bus-pass case, the dean asked for it.

Marsha didn't hand it to her. Instead, she said, she took out all the objects in it and gave them to the dean—her identification card, the working papers she needed for the after-school jobs she had held, a pass to the girl's washroom, and half a bus pass. Marsha hoped the dean wouldn't notice that partial bus pass. To save money, two students often split and shared a single pass; they knew a busy driver seldom noticed whether the card he was briefly shown was half a pass or a whole one. Using half a pass, of course, was one more punishable offense.

Dean Amicone didn't mention the half pass. She did, however, repeat the order to give her the bus-pass case.

"I gave you everything in it," Marsha told her.

Dean Amicone wasn't satisfied. She threatened to call the police, Marsha told Emery, if Marsha refused to give her the case.

Upset and growing angry, Marsha then threw the case toward the table. It slid off and fell to the floor in the corner of the small room. Dean Amicone ordered her to pick it up.

"You pick it up," Marsha answered.

But when Dean Amicone repeated her order, Marsha bent over, picked up the case, and handed it to her.

Dean Amicone looked through the empty case and then asked, "Where is it?"

"Where is what?" Marsha told Emery she replied.

Dean Amicone simply asked her the same question again.

"I was starting to get in a rage," Marsha told Emery. She said she sat down in silence, her hand clenched into a fist in her lap.

Dean Amicone, as calm as she had been all along, told her to open her fist. Marsha refused. And she continued to keep her fist clenched when the dean ordered her twice more to open it.

At this point the dean spoke through the open doorway to the secretary in the outer room, telling her to call for

Stephen Heitner, Bayside's security coordinator.

Heitner entered the inner office soon afterward, and he and Dean Amicone whispered together. Marsha remained seated, near tears now, her fist still tightly clenched.

Heitner turned to Marsha and asked her to open her hand.

"No," Marsha said.

He repeated the same order.

Marsha remained silent for a moment. Then, she told Emery, she asked Heitner, "Do you really want to see what's in my hand?" And she unclenched her fist and held up her hand, open and empty.

"And he just looked at me," Marsha recounted, "and Miss Amicone looked at me. Then they said something else to each other and then he said, 'We're going to have to call security.' And he told Miss Amicone they were going to have to search me."

Several minutes later Christine Gilbert entered the office, summoned by the walkie-talkie Heitner carried. Heitner left, closing the door behind him, but standing, as Marsha described it, "with his back like to the door, and you could see the shape of him through the glass."

Dean Amicone instructed Gilbert to search Marsha's coat. She told Marsha to remove her shoes and socks.

"I had on Earth shoes," Marsha told Emery. "Earth shoes, like natural shoes, and I had on a pair of white socks. So I took off my shoes and I took off my socks, and she took my shoes upside down. . . . She took my socks and she started going like this to my socks, right?" Marsha fingered imaginary socks in her hands.

Gilbert, searching Marsha's coat and then her books and book bag, asked Dean Amicone what it was she was supposed to be looking for. The dean ignored the question and instructed Marsha to remove her jeans.

"And I just looked at her, like. I'm getting upset and

starting to get nervous," Marsha told Emery, breaking into tears as she spoke.

"So I took off my dungarees," she went on, through her sobs. "She started going through my pocket, feeling the dungarees and everything. . . ."

After Dean Amicone had put the jeans on the table, she told Marsha to remove her top, a turtleneck sweater.

Marsha obeyed. "And when I took off my blouse I had on a bra that snapped in front," she said to Emery. "So she said to me, 'Marsha, unsnap your bra.' So I unsnapped my bra and everything, and I was getting ready to take it off. She said to me, 'No, no, you don't have to take it off,' like that. So I was standing there and crying. Then she said to me, 'Marsha, do you have anything in your panties?' I looked at her, right? I said to her—I said, 'Do you want to feel between my legs to see if I have anything in my panties?' She said to me, 'Just shut up and turn around and pull down your panties.' So I turned around, and I pulled down my panties, and I pulled them down to my legs and my back was toward her, and she pulled down my underwear. Then she said, 'You can put your clothes back on.' "

Marsha had dressed then, she said, picking up her shoes from the floor, her socks and dungarees and turtleneck from the table.

Emery asked what Christine Gilbert was doing while Marsha dressed.

"Standing near a bookcase," Marsha told him. "Like she was in a state of shock. Like she didn't know what to do."

Then, Marsha said, while she was putting her belongings back in her book bag—except for the half bus pass, which Dean Amicone had taken—the dean asked Gilbert to help her search the small room. They were still searching it when Dean Amicone told Marsha to go through the now-open door into the outer office. Marsha said Mr. Heitner was still there, along with a secretary and another security guard named Renee Weinberg.

Mrs. Weinberg had looked at the tears still streaming down Marsha's face. "She gave me a tissue," Marsha told Emery. And when Gilbert emerged from the inner room a few minutes later, she, too, came over to Marsha and suggested kindly that she comb her hair, which had been mussed by the turtleneck she had pulled over it. Gilbert also asked Marsha what it was they had been searching for.

"I told her I really didn't know." Marsha sobbed. But she added that not long afterward she did hear someone mention "a little white object."

Emery nodded. He knew Christine Gilbert's report had mentioned that she had eventually been told the search had been for something the dean had seen in Marsha's bus-pass case—a marijuana pipe, an object typically both small and white.

Next, Marsha said, Judith Sullivan, the dean to whom Marsha was officially assigned, came into the room. Dean Amicone spoke to her out of Marsha's hearing and showed her the half bus pass.

"Marsha, what did I tell you about this?" Dean Sullivan asked Marsha.

"I just looked at her," Marsha told Emery. "I wanted to jump up and smack her because I was so upset, and she was up there trying to tell me about something else. She didn't even know what happened."

Dean Sullivan had taken Marsha into her office, where she told her that after a hearing the next morning Marsha would be suspended for five days. Then the dean told her to take her things and go home.

She cried all the way home, Marsha told Emery. She couldn't stop. At home her older sister Natalie said the school had called about her suspension. "Mom is going to hit you," she told Marsha. The suspension, Natalie had been told, was because Marsha had stayed inside during a fire drill.

That night, instead of going to bed at ten as she usually did, Marsha waited until her mother came home after her hospital shift ended at eleven o'clock. She told Mrs. Martin the whole story.

While Marsha dried her eyes, Emery asked Mrs. Martin some questions. She said she had never seen her daughter as upset as she'd been that night, and that she'd been a changed girl from then on. Marsha no longer wanted to see her friends, Mrs. Martin said. She was withdrawn and kept to herself.

Emery asked Marsha if she could describe to him how the search had made her feel.

"Humiliated," Marsha said. "Dirty, disgusting, cheap, like an animal—and like a piece of property."

Before that day, she said, no one except her mother and her sister had ever seen her naked. She blamed herself for not having kept her clothes on, no matter what the dean had told her to do. She felt her family and friends blamed her, too, and either laughed at her or looked down on her for having let the search take place. Someone had even written on the wall of a Bayside girls' washroom that Marsha was "the bitch that got stripped." And there had been a rumor in the school that Marsha had been raped.

On the day after the search Mrs. Martin and Marsha had attended the hearing on Marsha's suspension. Neither Christine Gilbert nor Dean Amicone was present. Edmund Janko, Dean Sullivan, and the others who were there did not mention the search. Mrs. Martin tried to ask about it, after Marsha whispered to her to do so, but the school officials acted as if they didn't know what she was talking about. They were behaving, Mrs. Martin realized, as if the search had never occurred. Marsha was given a five-day suspension, and the meeting was adjourned without Mrs. Martin having had any further opportunity to press her questions.

Long after the suspension, Marsha had continued to be depressed and withdrawn. She felt she couldn't remain at Bayside High School after what had happened to her there. And so, with her mother's help, she transferred to another high school, where nobody knew her.

By the end of his first conversation with Marsha and her mother, Emery believed that Marsha's civil rights under the Fourth Amendment almost certainly had been violated. He knew that if the NYCLU took on her case—for which, of course, it would bear all the costs—its client's own misdemeanors would have to come out in court. Nevertheless, he felt Marsha deserved compensation for the indignity and humiliation she had suffered, from which she had not completely recovered and perhaps never could. It seemed to him that her case could have broader consequences, as well.

Emery's background gave him a special interest in the situation. After graduation from Brown University and Columbia Law School, and a year's clerkship with a federal judge, he had directed the state of Washington's Institutional Legal Services Project. That agency existed for the specific purpose of protecting the civil rights of hospitalized mental patients. But through his work with it, Emery was soon also representing prisoners and children in institutions, as well as the mentally retarded.

These people are all inmates of what are known legally as "closed" institutions—institutions in which people are confined by force or other effective means, and in which they have little or no control over their lives. Since Emery's recent arrival in New York to join the NYCLU staff, his concern had extended to the "inmates" of big-city schools. He felt that those schools, patrolled as they were by police and security guards, could well be considered "closed" institutions during the hours of the school day.

The other members of the NYCLU legal staff proved to be as interested in Marsha's case as Emery was. They all thought its successful outcome might establish new and more effective guidelines for shielding all public school students from illegal searches and for protecting their right to privacy.

Such new guidelines should be a welcome protection for school faculties, too, they agreed. Teachers and deans, informed specifically as to what they had the right to do to students or require a student to do, would be less likely in the future to face the possibility of the kind of lawsuit the NYCLU was now ready to set in motion.

Within days, Emery, acting for the NYCLU, filed suit in the United States District Court, Eastern District of New York, on behalf of the plaintiff, Marsha Martin, and her mother. Mrs. Martin was named in the court papers because Marsha was a minor. In those documents, Marsha was designated only by her initials in order to shelter her from the publicity that was bound to surround the trial. The defendants named in the suit were several school officials, including, of course, Dean Amicone and Stephen Heitner, who were responsible for the search.

Emery demanded money as damages for Marsha, and he expanded the suit to include two additional requests that went beyond Marsha's claim. The first of these requests—or pleas—was that the judge order the board of education to write new and less vague regulations for student searches, which would follow more closely the restrictions spelled out in the Fourth Amendment. The second request was that the judge declare Marsha's case a class action, on behalf of all other students who had been subjected to similar searches or who might undergo them in the future.

Marsha's damage suit would be decided by the judge and a jury. Emery's extra pleas would be decided by the judge alone.

The trial opened on a Monday, October 23, 1978, in the United States District Courthouse in Brooklyn, New York. The presiding judge, John F. Dooling, Jr., a man of nearly seventy, was known for his fairness and humanitarianism. Emery and a young assistant represented Marsha and her mother. The defendants were represented by the City of New York's lawyers.

During the nearly seven months since the NYCLU had filed the suit, Emery had acquired all the material he expected to need to plead Marsha's case. He had studied earlier cases that might have some bearing on this one, though there were relatively few involving school searches. He had subpoenaed relevant documents, such as Marsha's own class and conduct records, deans' reports, and the board of education's rules and regulations. He had interviewed all the people who would testify on Marsha's behalf—Marsha herself, her mother, Christine Gilbert, Renee Weinberg, students who had known Marsha at Bayside, and a psychiatrist who had interviewed her at length. And in a series of pretrial hearings, Emery—and opposing lawyers, as well—had questioned all the witnesses who would appear at the trial.

Statements made under oath at these hearings, called pretrial depositions, gave both sides a good idea of how the legal battle would shape up. Emery already knew, for example, that deans' records would be presented showing that Marsha had cut classes, smoked marijuana, been found with a split bus pass and with an ID card and bus passes that did not belong to her (she claimed she had been holding the latter for a friend), and been accused of stealing a fellow student's money (she claimed she had not taken it, and the theft had not been proved). Emery's opposition was going to try to show that Marsha was the kind of girl who could reasonably have been suspected of having a marijuana pipe in her possession and of having property in her book bag that she had stolen from other students' bags while she was alone in the English classroom during the fire drill. But Emery also knew that when Dean Amicone searched Marsha, beginning with a search of her book bag, nothing had been reported missing by any student in the English room. Therefore, Dean Amicone could not have had a reasonable suspicion that Marsha possessed stolen goods.

Emery suspected that the reasons the dean had nevertheless treated Marsha like a suspect were that she thought of Marsha as an impudent girl requiring discipline—and that Marsha was black.

Emery had been told there was racial prejudice at Bayside, and the recent change in the school's population made that seem not unlikely. Bayside's student body, nearly all white not long before, had become 38 percent black. But there were still only 3 black teachers among a faculty of some 170, and only 2 other blacks, including Christine Gilbert, on the nonteaching staff.

Emery put Marsha on the witness stand first. He asked her about her record of cutting classes, and she said she had sometimes done so. Most often, she said, she had cut the morning's brief attendance-taking session, because it seemed useless to her. Besides, she said, the teacher didn't like her. She admitted that she had smoked marijuana and that the school had told her mother about it and threatened her with suspension. She said she had never taken hard drugs and never would, because they frightened her. Once she had seen a boy she knew fall dead on the sidewalk from an overdose of hard drugs.

Finally, Emery guided Marsha through the story he had first heard in his own office. She had already repeated it for him seven or eight times since then, each time using almost exactly the same words and phrases, and beginning to cry at the same point at which she had started to cry in his office. Now, in court, she again told the story that had become so familiar to him, and began to cry once more when she described Dean Amicone's demand that she remove her clothes.

When Marsha reached the point in her story at which she was told to put on her clothes again, the court declared a brief recess. Afterward, when Marsha was calmer, Emery asked her some questions about the incident she'd described.

One of his questions was, "How did you feel after she told you to take off your jeans?"

"I was like—I was there and I was listening to everything she was saying," Marsha said, tense again, as if she were once more reliving that moment. "But like, it was like part of me was there and part of me wasn't there, because I was so upset and so nervous because I didn't know what to do. And I didn't know how to stop her. And I just didn't know what to do. I was like—I was almost in a state of shock at that point."

"And how was Miss Amicone—how was she when she asked you to take off your jeans?" Emery asked. "Can you describe her?"

"She was—like it was nothing," Marsha said. "She was all kind of calm and everything. She didn't raise her voice or like that. She just said, 'Marsha, take off your dungarees.'"

Marsha's testimony lasted all day. The next morning Emery called the psychiatrist, Dr. Eleanor Townsend, to the stand. Her credentials were impressive, and what she had to say about Marsha, after two lengthy interviews with her, echoed what Emery himself might have said about his young client.

Dr. Townsend described Marsha as a sensitive adolescent girl with

a history of trauma with violation of her sense of personal privacy, a feeling of degradation, a sense of grief and loss over the public exposure of her body and the assault on her self-esteem, and a sense of personal dignity. She had been made to feel guilty at her own compliant behavior and feels unable to make others understand her state of fear and sense of helplessness at the time of the search. . . . She shows signs and describes symptoms which are classical for victims of violence, be it robbery, burglary, assault or rape.

"In her account of being stripped and searched," Dr. Townsend added, "there is nothing exhibitionistic, only a sense of shame and outrage. . . . Marsha's grief and sorrow were entirely believable and her distressed crying was genuine."

Dr. Townsend concluded that without professional psychiatric help, Marsha might continue to be the loner she had become. She would be unable to rely on anyone except herself, because she had learned to distrust all other people.

That same day Marsha was called back to the stand to answer questions put by the opposing lawyers. Later the jurors were taken to Bayside High School to see for themselves the size of the small room in which Marsha had been searched—a room, Emery would claim, in which not even a small object could remain lost for very long.

On the third day of the trial, October 25, Emery questioned Marsha's mother first. Then he questioned Renee Weinberg, the security officer who had been puzzled by Marsha's tearful appearance after her search and had offered her a tissue to dry her eyes. Finally he questioned the personnel coordinator to whom Christine Gilbert had given the written report of Marsha's search.

On the fourth day, the distinguished Irving Anker took the stand. Dr. Anker had been serving as chancellor of the entire New York City school system at the time Marsha's search occurred. He said exactly what Emery wanted the jury to hear—that stripping a student was permissible only if a student's clothes had to be removed for the student's safety—if, for example, acid had been spilled on them.

Christine Gilbert, the security officer who had witnessed the search, testified that same day. Like some other witnesses, she pointed out that drug paraphernalia, which could be bought legally, was so common at Bayside that many girls and boys hung such things as pipes and spoons on their necklaces and bracelets. That was why she had been amazed to hear that a girl had been stripped to look for a single marijuana pipe.

Lester Speiser, the Bayside High School principal, followed Gilbert on the stand. Pressed by Emery, he said that to his knowledge Marsha had never carried a knife or a gun or possessed heroin, although other Bayside students had been found in possession of all those things. He also said that only once had she been found with marijuana and that, unlike certain other Bayside students, Marsha had never been arrested.

On the fifth day, Friday, there began a parade of defendants' witnesses. Mrs. Ragin, the English teacher in whose room Marsha had remained during the fire drill, said that Marsha had behavior problems, was often "emotionally distraught," but was intelligent and quite gifted in dramatics. Marsha had, in fact, been more interested in the study of *Julius Caesar* than any of her other students, she said. Only Marsha had been eager to try all the parts in the play, and she had been remarkably effective in all of them.

The purpose of Mrs. Ragin's testimony, Emery believed, was to suggest to the jury that Marsha, contrary to the psychiatrist's judgment, was definitely "exhibitionistic." Mrs. Ragin made it seem quite likely that a girl who could dramatize Shakespearean roles could also dramatize what had happened when she and the dean and Christine Gilbert had been together in that small room.

Edmund Janko, the dean of boys, testified next that he had caught Marsha hiding in the English classroom. He was followed by a teacher, an assistant principal, and two counselors, all of whom praised Dean Amicone's ability, her calm helpfulness, her good character, and her devotion to children. One of them described her as "concerned" for the students, and strict but fair.

The only other witness that day was Rosie Parris, president of the Bayside High School Parent-Teachers Association. She said there had never been any sign of racism at Bayside, and she warmly defended the school faculty. As a parent, she wanted teachers free to maintain security in the school by using whatever forms of discipline they thought necessary. "It is absolutely dangerous to tie the hands of responsible adults," she soon stated publicly, in an open letter to parent groups and school officials.

On Monday, after the weekend recess, Heitner, Dean Sullivan, and the assistant principal's secretary testified, repeating much of what the jury had previously heard. The next day Dean Amicone, an attractive, youthful woman with nineteen years of experience in the school system, took the stand.

She began her testimony with a list of Marsha's early misdemeanors at Bayside, some of which had already been testified to, in part by Marsha herself. Once, Dean Amicone said, she had found Marsha wandering in the hall, had sent her back to her classroom, and had discovered her a few minutes later in the cafeteria. She said Marsha's eyes had looked "glazed" that day. She suspected Marsha had been "high" on marijuana.

But such misdemeanors hadn't been the cause of her decision to search Marsha's bag on October 27, the dean said. That had been done, she declared, for Marsha's "own protection," in case she was later accused of taking anything that didn't belong to her while alone with other students' bags during the fire drill. She added that it was only when Marsha took the papers out of her bus-pass case, instead of obeying the dean's order to hand over thc case itself, that Dean Amicone had seen what then became the object of her search.

In an otherwise empty pocket of the case, Dean Amicone said, she had caught a quick glimpse of what she described as "a white instrument, a white pipe, a drug-related item."

"I saw a white pipe," she said she had told Marsha, and again asked for the case.

"I don't have to show you anything," she reported Marsha as answering. But when the dean repeated her request, Marsha had thrown the case toward the table, and it had fallen to the floor.

While bending over in the corner to pick up the case, after the dean had repeatedly told her to do so, Marsha was briefly out of the dean's sight. But, the dean said, she had observed Marsha putting her hands in her jeans, as if she were tucking her sweater into place.

"So I suspected that she had put it in her jeans," Dean Amicone went on, clearly meaning that she thought Marsha had hidden the white pipe. She had then sent for Heitner, and he had summoned Christine Gilbert as a witness.

To explain why she had not frisked the girl instead of asking her to remove her clothes, Dean Amicone said, "I did not want to touch Marsha. I know students are very, very sensitive about being touched. I know that. And so I thought that the lesser of two evils was to ask her to remove her jeans." Although, she said, before doing that she had repeatedly asked, "Marsha, really, why don't you give it to us?"

At that point, Dean Amicone said, Marsha had told her, "I'm going to tell my mother." And Dean Amicone said she had replied, "Well, of course, I expect you to tell your mother." In fact, Dean Amicone testified, she had persisted in her search so that she could show Mrs. Martin the pipe she had seen and thus convince her that Marsha was using drugs. Dean Amicone didn't mention—as Emery pointed out in his summation to the jury—that Mrs. Martin had prevously been shown a "joint" found in Marsha's locker. So why, Emery later asked the jury, "would you strip search somebody for something like that, to convince a mother of a matter that she had already been presented with some time before? It doesn't make sense. It's not true. That's why it doesn't make sense."

Dean Amicone then said she had not asked Marsha to remove her shoes and socks. ("We know she did," Emery later stated. "We know from Marsha and Christine Gilbert that the first thing she asked her to take off was her shoes and socks . . . and that's the only reasonable way to believe it happened.")

The dean also said she was surprised when she saw that, while she had been looking through Marsha's jeans, Marsha had—again without being asked—removed her sweater. (And this, too, Emery would ask the jury to consider: In such a small room, how could Marsha have gone through the vigorous gestures of pulling a turtleneck over her head without being noticed by a woman standing so near?)

"I was surprised and also embarrassed to see her that way," the dean testified, and said she had told Marsha to get dressed. But Marsha had asked if the dean wanted to

look through her bra and had started to open its front fas-
tener.

"I said, 'No, Marsha, that's not necessary. Turn
around,' " the dean told the jury. "I asked her to turn
around because I didn't want her to expose herself."

Marsha turned. And she was, the dean said, "mocking,
angry, vulgar—well, the statement was vulgar—anyhow,
she said, 'Do you want to look between my legs, Miss
Amicone?' And I said, 'No, Marsha. Get dressed.' . . . I
was shocked. I had not expected that. And my tone was a
strong, firm tone, to get dressed. I felt she was trying to
embarrass Ms. Gilbert and myself."

She was asked if Marsha had removed her panties. "She
went to pull them down in her anger, and saying, 'Do you
want to look between my legs?' " Dean Amicone testified.

Emery later disputed Dean Amicone's claim that Marsha, of her own volition, had brazenly removed her clothes
in order to "embarrass Ms. Gilbert and myself," as the dean
had put it. That Marsha would have done such a thing
was, he told the jury, "absolutely unbelievable."

In the summation to the jury he would also say, "It's
clear that no pipe existed in that room. You saw that room.
You couldn't lose a paper clip in that room. . . . There
was no white pipe." He would further claim that Dean
Amicone had a bias against Marsha because the girl was
impudent. The dean was "punishing her . . . punishing
her for her lack of respect," he would say.

"Is there more disrespect among students today than
there was when you began teaching?" he asked Dean
Amicone in his cross-examination.

Dean Amicone answered readily. Disrespect itself didn't
change, she explained, but the amount of it had increased
notably. Once a school might have perhaps four or five
disrespectful students to contend with; today that number

might be thirty or forty.

And had that increase in numbers begun to occur when Bayside started to change from a nearly all-white school to one with a student body that was 38 percent black? Emery asked her then.

Oh, yes, Dean Amicone told him. That was when it had begun.

Emery's final witnesses were three Bayside students who took the stand briefly. Their descriptions of the dean were not the same as those given by the dean's colleagues. One of the two girls said Dean Amicone was always trying to get people into trouble. The boy, who remarked casually that "all kids" had reefer paraphernalia, said he thought the girls found Dean Amicone "unpersonal."

"Impersonal?" Emery asked.

"Yes," the boy agreed, and said he didn't think the girls liked her much.

The fact-finding portion of the trial had ended. The next day, November 1, the opposing lawyers summed up their cases.

Emery did his best to present Marsha as a sensitive, insecure, occasionally troublesome girl, "both old and young at the same time . . . as all kids are who live in the city," a girl who had been subjected to an unjustified and humiliating strip search.

Urging the jurors to doubt Dean Amicone's testimony and the testimony of the faculty members who supported her, he said they were all chiefly interested in protecting their own reputation and that of the school. Their "loyalty to Bayside," he said, was "loyalty beyond the truth" and, to them, "more important than the truth."

The defendants' lawyer, in turn, did his best to portray Marsha as a troublemaker of long standing, a girl whose behavior on the day of the search had made that search a reasonable and therefore lawful exercise of school authority. He also repeated the PTA president's emphasis on the heavy responsibility school authorities bear for the safety and security of the students.

The following morning Judge Dooling delivered his charge to the jurors. Carefully he explained the laws, regulations, and constitutional rights involved in the case, to help them evaluate the conflicting testimony and points of view they had heard.

"Plaintiff and every other citizen," the judge said, "has a fundamental right secured . . . by the Fourth and Fourteenth Amendments to the Constitution, to be free, both with respect to their persons and their effects, from unreasonable searches and seizures.

"Students in a public school," he continued, "have that constitutional right, and the administrative or teaching personnel of the school may not, in the course of fulfilling their duty to maintain discipline . . . subject students to searches that are unreasonable."

A search would be unreasonable, the judge pointed out, unless it was prompted by "specific observations or reliably specific information, for example a theft in school of something that a student could conceal on his or her person or effects." Also, search would be unreasonable if it "was more intrusive than was warranted by the purpose of the search."

Judge Dooling wanted the jurors to understand the role of a school's administrators, as it applied to the case. He reminded them that during school hours they did perform, "to a limited degree, the duties of custodianship and conduct supervision that parents perform outside the school hours."

He also wanted them to understand Marsha's position.

Neither the fact that a student may have a poor scholastic conduct record, that the student at some time or times in the past may have been in possession of contraband or had a bus pass or I.D. card not her own, and that she remained in a classroom during a fire drill, nor all these taken together or standing by themselves justifies a search.

The judge was saying, in other words, that nothing in Marsha's past record of behavior could be used as a reason for searching her on October 27, 1977.

Then, to help the jurors before they retired for their deliberations on this admittedly complicated case, Judge Dooling gave them a list of questions requiring yes-or-no answers. He also gave them additional questions about the money damages Marsha should receive if they decided in her favor.

It was past three that afternoon when the jurors sent out word that they had reached a verdict. Judge Dooling and the lawyers returned to the courtroom, where Marsha and the defendants were waiting. When the jurors were seated once more in the jury box, the court clerk read to them the judge's first question: Did Dean Amicone have reasonable grounds for the search?

"Yes," the foreman replied. And he gave the same answer to the second question, which was like the first but referred to Heitner.

"Was the search unreasonably intrusive?" the clerk then asked.

"Yes," the foreman said.

It was a triumphant moment for Emery and his client. With the jury's decision that Marsha had undergone an unlawful, because unreasonably intrusive, search, she became entitled to money damages.

To both the fourth and fifth questions, however—as to whether Dean Amicone and Heitner had acted without malice and in good faith—the jurors also answered yes.

And this meant that Marsha would not be granted additional, or punitive, damages.

Then came the two questions that asked the jurors to sum up the general verdict they had arrived at. Was it in favor of Marsha, the plaintiff, or of the defendants?

"What is your verdict as between plaintiff and defendant Amicone?" the clerk asked.

"Amicone," the foreman replied.

"What is your verdict as between plaintiff and defendant Heitner?" the clerk asked.

"Heitner," the foreman answered.

The jury had decided the case against Marsha, in favor of Dean Amicone and Heitner.

The courtroom became utterly silent.

Finally, Judge Dooling addressed the jury's foreman. "Now, in your answer to question number three," he said, "—the question was: Was the search of the plaintiff unreasonably intrusive?—you answered that it was."

"Was unreasonable, yes," the foreman said.

"That it was unreasonably intrusive?" Judge Dooling repeated.

"Yes," the foreman said a second time.

"But you did not find any liability for that intrusive search. Is that right?"

"No," the foreman said. Jurors' heads nodded in agreement. No, they had not found any liability.

Again the courtroom was silent. The members of the jury seemed completely unaware of the inconsistency of a decision that declared the search unreasonably intrusive, but that at the same time declared Dean Amicone and Heitner innocent of any wrongdoing.

At that point, Judge Dooling could have directed liability in Marsha's favor—in other words, could have declared her eligible to receive damages for having been subjected to what the jurors had decided was an unreasonably intrusive search. Instead, he asked the jurors, "Would you mind returning to the juryroom while I discuss the verdict with counsel?"

With the jury out of the courtroom, the judge and the lawyers discussed means of clarifying a situation the jurors had apparently failed to understand. Then the jurors were called back, and the judge gave them further instructions and asked them to deliberate the case again. Because of the lateness of the hour, however, he adjourned court until the next morning.

During the following day, November 3, the jurors appealed once to the judge for still further clarification, and shortly afterward they announced that they had reached a new verdict. They had found a way to eliminate the judge's complaint about their first judgment. By simply changing their answer to the third question from yes to no, thus stating that the search had not been too intrusive, after all, they were able to declare without inconsistency that Dean Amicone and Heitner were not guilty.

Marsha had lost the case. She was not entitled to any damages. Dean Amicone and Heitner had been declared innocent, and thus they and all other deans and school authorities would be able to strip search students in the future with no more justification than had existed on October 27, 1977, at Bayside.

But Emery refused to accept the defeat. He immediately presented a motion asking the judge to reverse the jury's verdict, on the grounds that it was inconsistent with the evidence.

Emery knew how unusual his motion was. Judges are very unwilling to reverse a jury's verdict, to replace it with what is legally known as a "directed verdict." As Judge Dooling himself put it, "a directed verdict in Federal Courts is rare to the extreme, and a directed verdict for the plaintiff is rare among rare things."

That "rare among rare things," however, did occur. Scarcely more than a week later, Judge Dooling called the lawyers of both sides before him again and announced his decision.

He didn't order the board of education to write a new and less vague set of rules for the conducting of all future searches, as Emery had requested at the start of the trial. In the "complex school world," the judge said, it would be impossible to set up rigid rules that would apply to every case. Much could be done within the school, he said, "to systematize search procedures, and to create safeguards for teachers and students alike." But the initiative for it, he felt, "must not be imposed . . . by judicial intervention." He also refused Emery's plea to accept Marsha's case as a class action, on behalf of all students subjected to searches similar to hers.

But he did state flatly that, notwithstanding the jury's verdict, Marsha was entitled to damages. And in a long written version of his decision, issued later, he gave clear and detailed reasons for having done what so few judges had done before him.

"To justify searching a high school child for a possible stolen object," he wrote, "it is indispensable that there be a reliable report that something is missing, and not a report, however reliable, that the suspected student had an opportunity to steal." Since there had been no report of anything missing, he was saying, Marsha's "opportunity to steal" was of no consequence.

As for the body search, described by Dean Amicone as the search for a small white pipe, the judge said it was "so inordinate in terms of the object sought . . . that it cannot be defended on any ground." Even in school situations, he pointed out, where a reasonable suspicion was generally regarded as sufficient to justify an ordinary search, a teacher should have a stronger reason for a strip search. Before stripping a student, Judge Dooling said, a teacher should believe that it was not only reasonable but likely or probable that the student was hiding something on his or her person.

The judge was, in effect, ruling that school strip searches be carried out in close conformity with the Fourth Amendment. So, although he had denied Emery's two pleas—a denial Emery sought unsuccessfully to have reversed—the judge had granted much of what Emery had hoped to gain with them.

But it was still too early to rejoice over the chief victory Emery had won. The victory was not yet secure. Almost as soon as Judge Dooling's verdict was announced, the city's lawyers asked the United States Court of Appeals to reverse his ruling and reinstate the original jury verdict.

Lawyers for both sides prepared lengthy briefs to state their cases before the appeals court, bolstering their arguments with citations from previous decisions and books by recognized authorities in the fields of law and education. Emery, for example, referred to *In Re Gault* to strengthen his contention that educators, even those with the best of motives, must watch out lest in their zeal to do good they violate a student's basic civil rights.

Months went by. Finally, in late October of 1979, two years after Marsha had been searched and a year after the trial, the Court of Appeals handed down its verdict, according to which Marsha would receive $7,500 in damages.

In their one-page decision, the three judges unanimously upheld Judge Dooling. They said that teachers' "unique relationship to their students" did justify "flexibility when applying the Fourth Amendment" to searches in a school setting. But, they continued, "when a teacher conducts a highly intrusive invasion, such as the strip search in this case, it is reasonable to require that probable cause be present."

School teachers, deans, and principals all over the country recognized the importance of that decision. The judges who had written it represented only one of the eleven circuit courts of appeal in the United States. Nevertheless, as the *New York Times* pointed out, their court was "a frequent source of precedents that influence other states."

The *Times* quoted Richard Emery in that same story, whose headline said the court had "Set Restrictions on Strip Searches in High Schools."

"This is the highest court in the country to say that kids have these rights," Emery had said. "Teachers had better learn the law or face the probability of lawsuits and damages."

As for Marsha, Emery later told us, "I think she's going to be all right. She's doing well in school. She plans to go on to college in Virginia."

6

Invasion of Privacy

Is it possible to identify "potential drug abusers" among eighth graders and then remodel their personalities so that they don't become dependent on drugs? In 1972 a New Jersey psychologist, Fred Streit, said the answer to that question was yes.

Streit had recently conducted a drug-use survey for Pennsylvania's Montgomery County, which adjoins the city of Philadelphia. His report to the county commissioners had said that one out of every five Montgomery people between the ages of twelve and twenty-five was "heavily involved in drugs." The troubled commissioners were discussing rehabilitation programs for the drug users when Streit told them that too much time and money already had been spent on such programs, many of which had failed. On the other hand, he said, far too little was spent for the prevention of drug use. He then proposed that the county use a "preventive" approach to the problem, which he said could effectively reduce the number of drug users among high school students. And he said he had devised such a program.

Data collected during the recent county survey, Streit said, showed a "failure pattern" among users of heroin, barbiturates, and alcohol. From this he had concluded, as he put it, that "an almost positive sign of a potential drug user is a very negative self-image." His plan was to "identify" students with a poor self-image and, by means of an "intervention team," help them change that image. The "identification" would be done through "tests," or questionnaires, given to eighth-grade students and their teachers.

The eighth-grade group had been chosen, Streit explained, because those students had reached a year he saw as a "critical period of human development, manifesting itself at the biological, psychological and social levels of development." He also saw that year as a period when young people were more susceptible than they previously had been to influences outside their homes. Thus potential drug abusers, recognized during the eighth grade, would be open to help offered by an "intervention team."

The team would be made up of a school administrator, teachers known to be sympathetic to students, other students whose tests had shown them to have good self-images, and various experts—drawn from outside the school system, if necessary—such as psychologists and psychiatrists. All members of the team, except for the experts, would be given a brief course of instruction to prepare them for the program.

The name Streit gave his program was Critical Period of Intervention, a cumbersome phrase usually reduced to the initials CPI. The student test he planned to use, Streit said, was different in one important way from any tests previously devised for similar use. It included questions about a student's attitudes toward his or her parents, which Streit regarded as important clues to the kind of self-image acquired during a young person's early years.

The commissioners were impressed. At a September 1972 meeting, they made plans to introduce a pilot CPI program into three of Montgomery County's school districts—Norristown, Wissahickon, and Lower Merion. They felt they had made a wise decision, one that would benefit the youth of the county.

Joan Gluckman of Norristown was present at that meeting. Because she was interested in and involved in the affairs of her community, she often attended the meetings of elected officials, which were open to the public but usually ignored by it. What she heard at this one left her amazed and shocked.

Very little was said about the actual workings of the CPI plan, of which the public then knew nothing. But to Mrs. Gluckman the tests that were mentioned sounded as if they would flagrantly violate a student's right to privacy. Her immediate reaction was that the ACLU—she was an officer of its local branch—should find out more about the plan in order to be able to defend any civil rights it might endanger.

She therefore sent a report of the meeting to the ACLU's Greater Philadelphia office. She also saw to it that a newsletter went out to members of the Norristown ACLU unit, alerting parents to the program that was scheduled to be carried out in their school. The letter recommended that they refuse to let their children take the CPI tests until full information about the whole program was supplied to them. The local ACLU would give them any help possible, the letter said.

Gluckman also alerted Sylvia Merriken, a civic-minded friend who often attended public meetings with her but had missed the one at which CPI had been mentioned. Mrs. Merriken, a trained nurse, worked with a hospital's drug-rehabilitation program. She was thus acutely aware of the dangers of drug abuse and of the painful social ostracism drug addicts could suffer. It disturbed her that any young person might be required to take a test that could result in the label "potential drug addict." If that was what would happen under the CPI plan, she said, she would strongly oppose its use in the Norristown school. Michael, oldest of her three children, was in that school's eighth grade.

In the meantime Spencer Coxe, director of the ACLU's Greater Philadelphia office, was attempting to obtain a copy of "Preventive Approach," a paper in which Fred Streit described his plan. Some days went by before Coxe succeeded and could read the paper. It left him, he said, "outraged." But he wanted experts' opinions of it, so he sent copies to a psychiatrist and a group of psychologists. He also hoped to find out more about the plan and how the school districts meant to use it. In a letter to one of his consultants he set down what little he had been able to learn by then. His letter said:

In Norristown, we are told, the tests will be given in October to all school children, without prior notification of the parents. In the Wissahickon School District, our information is, they plan to administer the tests to a smaller number of children, and also get parental permission before doing so. The other school district that apparently has agreed is Lower Merion, and we don't know what their plans are.

It was through the superintendent of the Lower Merion Junior High School that Coxe shortly thereafter saw a copy of the actual tests to be given to students and their teachers. The Lower Merion superintendent did plan to use them, after informing the students' parents. Out of concern for students' civil rights, however, he had already sought advice from a lawyer who had worked with the ACLU, and the lawyer had found no fault with the tests. The superintendent was willing to show them to Coxe, in the hope that they would change his opinion of Streit's program. But Coxe's reaction to the four-part student test—which students would be told to sign—and the one to be administered to their teachers was an even greater sense of outrage than he had felt before.

The first part of the students' test asked about the race and religion of the student's family; whether the student lived with one or both parents or with neither; and the number of the student's siblings, if any. Also, it told the student to choose one of four given phrases to answer the question: "How would you describe your family?" The choices were:

1. We are very close.
2. We are somewhat close.
3. We are not too close.
4. We are not close at all.

In the test's second part, the student was given five

groups of phrases and asked to select one in each group to answer the question: "Which of these four students is MOST LIKE YOU?" One of the groups was:

1. Someone who will probably be a success in life.
2. One who gets upset when faced with a difficult school problem.
3. Someone who has lots of self-confidence.
4. A student who has more problems than other students.

Another group was:

1. A student who is well liked.
2. One who makes unusual or odd remarks in class.
3. Someone who has lots of common sense.
4. One who has to be coaxed or forced to work with other students.

The next part of the test consisted of the same phrases the student had already read, but grouped differently. And this time one phrase in each group was to be chosen to answer the question: "Which of these four students is LEAST LIKE YOU?" For example:

1. One who makes unusual or odd remarks in class.
2. A student who is good in school work.
3. Someone who is interested in things he can do alone.
4. Someone who will probably be a success in life.

The instructions for the next part of the test began, "We are interested in learning more about the different experiences people have had in their families." It consisted of more than a hundred incomplete statements, with four boxes beside each one. The boxes represented, in order: mother and father; mother only; father only; and neither parent. Each statement had to be completed by checking one of those boxes. The student was told to indicate, for example, whether both parents, only one of them, or neither of them "Hugged and kissed me when I was small."

Among the other statements to be completed in the same way were:

Tell me how much they love me.
Are very strict with me.
Make me feel I'm not loved.
Don't give me any peace until I do what they say.

The final part of the test made use of the same twenty phrases used previously, but now the phrases appeared singly. Beside each one, the instructions said, the student should write the name of a classmate "who is *most like* or *often like* the student described." The student taking the test was thus asked to name a fellow student who was, for example, "Someone who makes unusual or odd remarks in class" and "A student who has more problems than other students."

The test to be given to eighth-grade teachers asked them to supply students' names, too. They were to write the names of the one or two students in each of their classes who were "most like" and "least like" the individuals described in eight statements. Among the statements were:

This pupil has to be coaxed or forced to work or play with other pupils. He or she will actively avoid having any contact with classmates.
This pupil makes unusual or inappropriate responses during normal school activities. His behavior is unpredictable.
This pupil behaves in ways which are dangerous to self or others. This pupil will get into situations in which he or she may be hurt or frightened.

"The information you provide when completing this form will be kept CONFIDENTIAL," the instructions to the teachers said. "You are not labeling a child when you answer these questions. The information will become part of a data bank on each child to enable us to provide the kind of help necessary to predict difficulties and prevent them from happening."

On October 5, Joan Gluckman attended another meeting of the county commissioners. There she presented the ACLU's official views on the plan, which Coxe, his expert consultants, and others had now been able to study. The Philadelphia *Bulletin* reported the meeting under the headline "ACLU HITS PLAN TO SPOT PUPIL DRUG POTENTIAL."

"The entire scheme," Gluckman was quoted as saying, "is based on the dubious assumption that students who vary from what the testers consider the norm are in danger of falling into drug abuse." The ACLU, she had told the press, was prepared to furnish legal assistance to pupils or parents who chose to challenge what she called "this gross abuse of the school's power" and "an outrageous invasion of privacy."

The story aroused the curiosity of a public until then uninformed about—almost unaware of—the county commissioners' decision to introduce Streit's CPI program into the county schools. To satisfy that curiosity, the commissioners held a press conference a few days later, and a dozen media representatives covered it.

Streit was present to answer questions. The next day's newspapers quoted him as saying that while current drug programs were not working, his CPI plan offered a really effective method to reduce drug use. When asked about the CPI tests, he would say only that they required students to rate their attitudes toward their parents, their peers, and themselves.

One of the commissioners had said that CPI was so designed that it would "allow the school to center its reme-
dial program on those in need of help, rather than running basically ineffective mass drug educational classes."
Another commissioner had said, "We don't know if it will
work, but something has to be done. I don't feel we can
be negative about dealing with our children." And he had
added, "We are trying to do a job we haven't been able to
do in the past."

Some reporters, still puzzled, had asked if they might
see copies of the tests. Streit had firmly refused. If the
tests were made public, he said, they would then have
little or no value.

Spencer Coxe had made a point of attending the press
conference and had repeated the ACLU's evaluation of the
CPI program for the reporters. "Its only beneficiaries," he
had declared, "will be the researchers who need the
schools to provide guinea pigs for their studies."

The director of the county drug commission, who was
also at the conference, had taken strong exception to
Coxe's statement. "This commission," he had said, "has
responded to a need that was initiated by this county and
has attempted to do something about it."

At the end of the conference a reporter had asked Coxe
if the ACLU planned to take legal action in the matter.
"Litigation depends on whether or not we find out from
the school districts that they are going to go ahead with
this," Coxe had answered. "We've been asked by two parents to stop the program. If we decide to go ahead, we
would sue the school districts and the county commissioners."

One of the parents Coxe was referring to was Sylvia
Merriken, mother of eighth-grader Michael Merriken. She
had discussed the subject with Michael before making any

other move. Unlike her two younger children, Michael didn't usually say "Oh, Mother! Must you?" when she became involved in a public protest or a campaign for a cause she believed in. He always seemed to understand, she thought. And he certainly understood now. He realized he could be brought into any legal action she might take in connection with the CPI plan. But he could see why she opposed it and was willing to support her stand.

So Sylvia Merriken conferred with Judah Labovitz, a parent himself and member of a prominent Philadelphia law firm. Labovitz had volunteered to take on various ACLU cases in the past. Now he was more than willing to volunteer again because he, too, was appalled by the CPI plan. He drew up the necessary papers for a suit against the Norristown Board of Education on behalf of both Merrikens, Sylvia and Michael.

Another prominent lawyer member of the ACLU, however—a woman who had long been active in parent organizations in the Lower Merion School District—was taking a very different attitude toward the situation. In a sharply worded letter to Spencer Coxe she charged him with "hysteria," from which, she wrote him, "no cause profits . . . and certainly not the cause of civil liberties.

"The ACLU certainly had the obligation to bring to the attention of our School Board the serious nature of the problems associated with the prospective drug study," her letter said. But it also said that the public exposure Coxe had given the program, and his recommendation to parents "to participate in a mass protest at a School Board meeting" were "completely uncalled for."

Opinion outside the ACLU was beginning to be as clearly divided as that inside the organization. An editorial in a local newspaper, under the heading "PREVENTING DRUG ABUSE . . . WHY THE OPPOSITION?" warmly commended the county commissioners for "their willingness to come to grips with the desperate need." The commissioners' plan, it said, "deserves positive support from parents and the general public as well.

"It is difficult to appreciate the opposition that is forming to it—principally from the American Civil Liberties Union," the editorial went on. The writer found it "hard to see how anyone's civil rights will be violated," and called the ACLU's opposition "a dangerous threat to a program that does have a positive thrust."

But growing numbers of parents and other citizens were now questioning the value of the CPI plan, as information about it seeped out into the three communities immediately involved.

"They're saying now that parents can tell their kids not to take the test, if they want to," one father said. "But what happens if just one parent tells his kid not to take it? Won't that kid get laughed at, or be made to look peculiar?"

"What's this 'confidentiality' the schools talk about?" another parent asked.

They say all the answers on the tests will be kept confidential, but they also say the information will be used by teachers and psychologists and others on what they call their "intervention team." And who's to say those people won't hand it out to others—to a curious cop, maybe, or to someone who's thinking about hiring a kid for a summer job?

Suddenly the school board of the Lower Merion School District announced that it was withdrawing its district from the CPI program. The president of a parents' organization there, who said the "intrusion" of the ACLU into the situation had been "unfortunate," added that confusion and lack of communication between parents and schools had been chiefly responsible for the whole "sorry history of events."

That lack of communication, Coxe was always ready to point out, was the very reason the ACLU had made the moves it had. "We do not apologize for bringing to the attention of the public what it is the public's right to know," he was soon writing the Lower Merion lawyer who had recently charged him with hysteria.

In the meantime, while Judah Labovitz planned the suit on behalf of the Merrikens, Spencer Coxe and his consultants held meetings with school superintendents and school boards, sometimes with Streit present. Advocates of the CPI plan seemed eager to make changes that might win over those who opposed it. Streit, for example, removed from the first section of the students' test the questions on a student's race and family religion. School officials revised the letters they now said would be sent to all parents before the tests were given, so that the tests would be more clearly "voluntary." A parent would no longer have to write the school in order to remove a child from the test program; instead the test would be given only to those students whose parents specifically requested a child's participation in CPI.

But the essentials of the program remained unchanged. On October 19, therefore—during the week when testing had originally been scheduled to begin in the three school districts—Judah Labovitz filed the Merrikens' suit in the U.S. District Court of Eastern Pennsylvania. The defendants were the nine members of the Norristown Area School Board and the principal of the junior high school. Michael and the principal, Wilmer D. Cressman, gave the case the name by which it would be known in the law books: *Michael Merriken et al.* v. *Wilmer D. Cressman et al.*, or, more briefly, *Merriken* v. *Cressman*.

In addition to bringing the suit, which asked the permanent abandonment of the CPI plan in the Norristown school, Labovitz also asked the court for a preliminary injunction—a ruling that would prevent the use of the program until the suit could be settled. The ruling, however, proved unnecessary. Norristown school officials volunteered not to go forward with the CPI plan until after the suit had been heard in court. And officials of Wissahickon, the third district involved in the program, announced that that district, too, would delay testing until after the hearing.

One county official, a supporter of the CPI plan, told the press:

If the court finds that there are civil rights violations, the program is stopped for this year. We would want it stopped ourselves if there are any such violations in it, for we are concerned about children's civil rights. We will change the program if there are violations.

I myself don't see how there could be. It is a voluntary program with parental consent as well as the children's own agreement necessary before any participation. How can a voluntary program invade privacy?

Sylvia Merriken, interviewed by a local newspaper, gave her own opinion of the "voluntary" quality of the program. The letter she herself had received from the Norristown district superintendent, she said, had arrived on October 13—that is, before the CPI program had been widely publicized. "It was a brief, vague letter," she recalled. "If we didn't want our child to take the test, we were to contact the principal. That was all. The whole thing was played down to the point where you could be unaware of the implications, because of a lack of complete information."

She was still disturbed that a child might be labeled a

"potential drug addict" because of answers he might give on a test. And because she had seen a copy of the student test, she had other concerns, as well. "It asks the children to give classmates' names to match certain characteristics," she told the reporter, and pointed out the dangers beyond that of asking a child to "tattle" on another. "A child can lie because he is angry at a friend," she said. "He can put the name of a classmate he dislikes."

As to the confidentiality of the test, she said, "No matter how confidential they say the tests would be, a child has to know he has been labeled a potential drug addict simply from the help he is getting after the tests are evaluated."

The child would also realize that others knew about the label, and Sylvia Merriken regarded the possible result of this as one of the greatest dangers of the program. "The child could easily say," she said, " 'Okay, if that's what they think, I might as well be a drug addict.' " She felt, in other words, that the child, aware that his peers and elders saw no better future for him than drug abuse, might turn to drugs as a result.

After the announcement of the suit, news reporters tried once more to obtain copies of the test materials. The district court judge who was scheduled to hear the case thwarted their effort by issuing an order that the tests not be made public. Several newspapers intervened, describing the judge's order as censorship of the press.

Then, on the grounds that his son's connection with Montgomery County officialdom might make him appear to have a conflict of interest in the matter, that judge offered to withdraw from the case. His offer was accepted by both parties to the suit. And Judge John M. Davis, named in his place, immediately reversed the secrecy order protecting the test materials.

At about the same time, Labovitz broadened the Merriken case into a class action so that the suit would represent not only the Merrikens but all students who might be tested in a Norristown CPI program. And—because the program would be paid for out of Montgomery County funds—he added the county's taxpayers to the class, as well.

Once the tests became available to the press, the public learned something about their contents. One local newspaper editorial posed some of the test questions to its readers and warned them, "Think carefully before you answer. If you are not careful, you could find yourself labeled a potential drug user." The editorial added, "No one faults the board's intentions. There are preventive programs in the field of physical health. Why not in mental health too? . . . The fault," it concluded, "lies not in the purpose but in the method."

The Merriken suit came before Judge Davis in December. Michael Merriken's testimony lent dramatic weight to his mother's fears about the harm that could be done to a young person "identified" as a "potential drug abuser." Michael, of course, had not taken the CPI test. But when news of the suit became known in the Norristown school, Michael had been subjected to painful jibes from other students.

"Are you a junkie, Mike?" he told the court one of them had asked loudly, in the presence of others. "Is that why your mother doesn't want you to take the test—because she's afraid of what it will show up about you?"

A psychiatrist, testifying on the Merrikens' behalf, was not surprised by Michael's evidence about his fellow students' reaction. Asked about the protection offered by the "voluntariness" of the student test, he said that any child refusing to take the test would indeed run the risk of being compared to an alleged criminal refusing to take the stand during his own trial. Such a refusal, although fully protected by the Constitution, is frequently interpreted by the public as an admission of guilt.

Judah Labovitz, the Merrikens' lawyer, took care to cover all aspects of the CPI program in his presentation of their case. He spoke about the treatment designed for the identified potential drug abusers. Each "identified" student, he said, would be assigned to a "peer group." The group's announced purpose was to alter "deviant behavior." But, he pointed out, members of the group would not be told what "deviant behavior" was—they would be expected to decide that for themselves.

"Deviancy," he quoted Streit as having written, "is painstakingly defined and discouraged by the group itself. It can include not only socially proscribed behavior, but any action which violates the group's specific normative system." Those who violated the group's "system," as Streit called it, could expect to be punished, Labovitz went on. He then read to the court Streit's description of the various punishments that might be meted out: "work details, withdrawal of privileges, recommendation to a special unit for intensive training, or the assignment of more onerous . . . tasks."

Labovitz made his own opinion of that part of the program clear by saying it showed "very close similarities" to the way people were controlled in George Orwell's famous novel, *1984*. In that book everyone is watched at all times by the electronic eye of "Big Brother" and punished for any behavior that does not meet with its approval.

But Labovitz addressed the court with special fervor on two other aspects of the CPI programs. One was portions of the tests that, he said, "invade the right of free speech and chill the exercise of those rights." He pointed out that there, "Both students and teachers are asked to identify those members of the class who 'make unusual or odd remarks.' " Then he added that, again, no guidelines were given to judge "what is or is not an odd or unusual remark." Is a student guilty of making such a remark, he asked, if he or she "supports an unpopular cause such as abortion, or an unpopular political candidate such as a member of the Communist party? . . ."

If a student realized that expressing unpopular points of view might lead to "identification as a potential drug abuser," Labovitz said, that student might well decide to "keep his thoughts and his ideas to himself. . . . Thus political dissent, differences of opinion, open academic inquiry will be chilled and stifled in the very citadel in which they should be protected and encouraged."

The other aspect of the CPI program against which Labovitz argued most strongly involved the student test questions he described as "highly personal . . . including many which, in the usual course of events, are not considered to be the business of the schools. . . . The CPI questionnaire asks whether the child's family is very close, somewhat close, not too close, or not close at all." That question, and the many others that asked the child "intimate things" about his parents, represented, Labovitz declared, an invasion of the right of privacy.

"There can no longer be any serious question that within the first nine amendments to the Constitution there is an inherent right of privacy which is equally binding upon the states," he said, adding that the Supreme Court had declared that the right extended to family relationships.

"There can be absolutely no question that the CPI program intrudes massively into that very area of constitutionally protected privacy," he went on.

If adults were compelled to fill out sheets with their names at the top, to be exposed to total strangers, asking intimate questions about their own relationships, including intimacies shared in the privacy of the home and in the bedroom, no one would doubt the invasion of privacy implicit in such a procedure. . . . The hallway between the parents' room and the child's room within the home is no less sacrosanct than the marital bedroom itself, and defendants should not be able to invade that protected domain of privacy.

"Plaintiffs therefore request," Labovitz concluded, "that an injunction be issued restraining defendants from implementing the CPI program."

On September 28, 1973, almost a year after the program had first come to the attention of the ACLU and Sylvia Merriken, Judge Davis's decision on the case was published. It read:

Defendants, their agents, servants and employers and all persons acting in concert with them are permanently enjoined and restrained from implementing or in any other way proceeding with the CPI program and from expending any further county or school district revenues on the CPI program.

His decision, echoing many of the points made in Labovitz's brief, answered a number of the questions that had arisen about a case that had won considerable and widespread publicity. The judge referred to the "good intent and motive" of the defendants and spelled out at some length the reasoning behind his decision against them.

Two of the program's specific dangers, as he described them, were "the risk that the CPI Program will operate as a self-fulfilling prophecy in which a child labeled as a potential drug abuser will by virtue of the label decide to be that which people think he or she is anyway"; and "scapegoating, in which a child might be marked out by his peers for unpleasant treatment, either because of refusal to take the test or because of the results of the test.

"When a program talks about labeling someone as a particular type, and such a label could remain with him for the remainder of his life," he went on, "the margin of error must be almost nil."

Referring to what had been legally called a "balancing test," he explained this meant that

the Court balances the invasion of privacy against the public need for a program to learn about and possibly prevent drug abuse in a society which has become highly aware of its dangers. . . . If the Court finds the public need so great and the invasion minimal, then it could sanction the Program in favor of public need.

But the court had found otherwise in this case. "As the Program now stands, the individual loses more than society can gain in its fight against drugs," the judge declared.

The judge had decided against the defendants because he had found the CPI program an invasion of the right to privacy—a right he said "should be treated with as much deference as free speech." The specific right to privacy that he meant his ruling to protect was that between parent and child. "There probably is no more private relationship, excepting marriage, which the Constitution safeguards," he wrote.

Sylvia Merriken and her son Michael, and the ACLU of Greater Philadelphia, had won a case that would strengthen students' right to privacy in every school in the country.

7

Free Speech and Free Press on Campus

If a student newspaper editor is told that something he or she has written can't be published because it is out of line with school policy, and that decision is accepted without protest, probably only the editor's friends will ever hear about the incident. But if the student editor does protest—and protests effectively—the result may become known far and wide.

That happened in 1967, when Gary Dickey, a junior at Alabama's Troy State College, protested the faculty censorship of an editorial he had written for the school newspaper. With the help of the Alabama affiliate of the ACLU, his protest took the form of a much-publicized court case— *Dickey* v. *Alabama State Board of Education.*

Like most students at Troy State—which is located in the small town of Troy, some fifty miles south of Alabama's capital, Montgomery—Dickey lived not far from the college. His home was in nearby Plattville. But Dickey, who was a junior in 1967, was not a typical Troy student in other respects.

Older than most of them—he was twenty-four—he was a decorated veteran of the Vietnam War. He had attended college for a year in Florida before transferring to the magnolia-shaded Troy campus. By early spring of his junior year he was one of its outstanding students. He was copy editor of the school's yearbook, editor-in-chief of Troy's literary magazine and its student handbook, and staff member of the *Tropolitan,* the school's weekly newspaper. Also, since the *Tropolitan* editor's recent resignation, Dickey was one of three students responsible for putting out the paper until a new editor could be named in a mid-April election.

In March of that year Dickey became convinced that the *Tropolitan* should take an editorial stand on a controversy being discussed throughout the state. Dr. Frank Rose, president of the prestigious University of Alabama, had been attacked by certain members of the state legislature for not censoring a university student publication called "Emphasis '67: A World in Revolution." And when Dr. Rose persisted in his defense of what he regarded as the students' right to academic freedom, the legislature's disapproval of him had become intense.

The publication that had aroused the legislators' anger, Dickey explained in the editorial he wrote for the *Tropol-*

itan, had been prepared in connection with a program of talks and panel discussions held at the university. Along with brief biographies of the participants in the program, it contained excerpts from some of their speeches. The participants had included Secretary of State Dean Rusk; General Earl G. Wheeler, chairman of the Joint Chiefs of Staff; and the known "revolutionaries" Bettina Aptheker, a Communist, and Stokely Carmichael, well-known advocate of black power.

"Some of the legislators have read into this publication an attempt by President Rose to condone and abet revolutionary and subversive activity at the University," Dickey's editorial said. "The *Tropolitan* feels that these legislators have sadly misinterpreted the intent of the publication.

"Surely," his editorial continued,

they cannot seriously consider Gen. Wheeler, the highest military official in the United States, a subversive. Surely Secretary of State Dean Rusk, who was brought to the University as the keynote speaker on the "Emphasis" program, and who is currently conducting a war of diplomacy and bullets against Communist subversion in Asia, cannot be labeled a subversive. The very purpose of including excerpted speeches by revolutionaries Carmichael and Aptheker was not to endorse their views, but to present a backdrop against which the phenomenon of revolution could be defined.

Dickey concluded:

The *Tropolitan,* therefore, laments the misinterpretation of the "Emphasis" program by members of the legislature, and the considerable harassment they have caused Dr. Rose. It is our hope that this episode does not impair his effective leadership at the University or discourage him in his difficult task.

The title Dickey chose for his editorial was "A Lament for Dr. Rose."

Like all material used in the *Tropolitan,* the editorial had to be submitted to the student newspaper's faculty adviser, Wallace Waites. Waites read it through and shook his head. It couldn't be published, he said.

"Why not?" Dickey asked.

"It might not meet with Dr. Adams's approval," Waites told him.

Dickey knew that Dr. Ralph Adams, president of Troy State College, had been angered not long before by an editorial Waites had approved. "Get that damn paper straightened out," President Adams was reported to have told Waites then.

So Dickey understood Waites's reluctance to arouse the president's disapproval again. But Dickey also knew that the woman who recently had resigned as editor of the *Tropolitan* had done so in protest against censorship by the administration. He therefore took his editorial to Dr. Phillip Wade, Waites's superior as head of the college's English department. And Wade, who shared Dickey's sympathy with Dr. Rose and his opposition to censorship, not only approved of the editorial but put his opinion in writing.

"Take your editorial back to Waites," he told Dickey, "and show him what I think of it. Tell him it should be published."

Waites, however, would not change his mind. "Wade has authority over me in my classroom work," he pointed out, "but none whatsoever in my direction of the *Tropolitan.*"

Dickey then took his editorial to the college president himself. President Adams's reaction was immediate: It was not to be published.

"Would you tell me why?" Dickey asked.

"Because the editor of a paper should not criticize the paper's owner," President Adams said. And he defined the *Tropolitan*'s owner as "Governor Wallace, acting in capacity of owner for the state, the state legislature, and the college board of trustees."

The governor of Alabama at that time was Lurleen Wallace—Mrs. George Wallace. She had succeeded her husband the year before, when he had been prohibited by law from running for a second term. But George Wallace, by that time preparing to run for the presidency of the United States, was still Alabama's governor in everything but name. President Adams was an ardent admirer of his, and this was not the first time that Adams had enforced what was coming to be known as the "Adams Rule": that no one connected with Troy State could criticize "the governor" or the Alabama legislature.

When Dickey returned to the *Tropolitan* office, Waites instructed him to use another editorial in place of his own. Chosen from material the *Tropolitan* regularly received from an organization of college newspaper editors, the substitute Waites handed him was called "Raising Dogs in North Carolina."

Instead of obeying Waites, Dickey gave instructions of his own to the *Tropolitan*'s printer. On the editorial page of the paper's next edition there would appear the headline, "A LAMENT FOR DR. ROSE," and below it there would be a large blank space slashed diagonally by the word *Censored*.

Dickey took one more step to express his protest against what had happened. He sent a copy of his editorial to the Montgomery *Advertiser*, the state capital's leading newspaper.

On April 8 the *Advertiser* printed it, in full, on a front

page devoted almost entirely to what was going on at Troy State College. On that page there was also a reproduction of the *Tropolitan*'s editorial page, with its blank space marked *Censored,* and a letter in support of Dr. Rose sent to the paper by thirty-five Troy students.

"We are proud to be students of Troy State College and citizens of Alabama," that letter said. "However, we feel that under the present administration, both at the college and state level, the proper atmosphere for academic learning and freedom has been suppressed and endangered by the prevailing feeling exhibited by our leaders."

The student letter writers had requested that their names not be printed "for fear of the termination of our scholastic careers at Troy State College."

The major story on the *Advertiser*'s front page, written by the paper's city editor, appeared under a five-column-wide headline that declared "PRO-ROSE EDITORIAL IS CENSORED AT TROY." The story quoted President Adams as saying, in a telephone interview, that

The *Tropolitan* enjoys more freedom of the press than many other papers in the country. The only restriction is that an editor or writer should not criticize the owner. Many papers have rules other than that. At Troy State, writers and editors have had wide freedom to criticize professors, school policy, activities and most any other subject or person. But I do feel they should not criticize the owner.

The *Advertiser* also reported that a group of Troy professors—all members of the American Association of University Professors—had issued a statement in defense of Dr. Rose. They had invited Dickey to show them his editorial, had agreed that it should have been published, and had appointed a committee to investigate the censorship. The English department head, Dr. Wade, was quoted as saying that he personally had endorsed the editorial and "didn't think any punitive action would be taken" against Dickey. The story concluded with expressions of support for Dr. Rose from the Montgomery County Board of Education, the students of the University of South Alabama, and the Alabama chapter of Sigma Delta Chi, the organization of professional journalists.

The following week the *Advertiser* was again reporting events at Troy State. One was a special meeting of the Student Government Association, at which a resolution had been offered expressing displeasure with President Adams's censorship and calling on the college administration to "insure that freedom of the press, and particularly freedom of the *Tropolitan,* shall forever be granted at Troy State College."

Only the association's senators were empowered to vote on the resolution. Six of them abstained, but the resolution passed nineteen to four.

President Adams had been present at the meeting but had not spoken. The next morning he gave a statement to the *Tropolitan,* whose publication that day had to be held up for two hours in order to include it. He had declared that the student and faculty meetings held to protest his censorship of Dickey's editorial—meetings that, he pointed out, he had not prohibited—were in themselves proof that "true academic freedom" existed at Troy State. Asked if he meant that he would no longer censor material in the *Tropolitan,* he replied, "No comment."

That same day it became known that Dickey had been refused permission to run for election to the post of *Tropolitan* editor. The decision had been made by the Student Publications Board, consisting of three officials of the administration and four students. The reason given for Dickey's exclusion from the list of approved candidates was that his average grade was "slightly below" the 85 required of anyone holding the editorial post.

The possibility of a write-in vote for Dickey was rumored about campus. In response to the *Advertiser*'s query as to whether Dickey could in fact become editor if he were elected by such means, President Adams's response was another "No comment."

Only 291 of the college's some 3,000 students exercised their right to vote in the election for the *Tropolitan*'s editor. Of that number, 44 wrote in Dickey's name. Three other write-in candidates received one vote each. The winner, with 184 votes, was a *Tropolitan* staff member who had been on the officially approved list of candidates.

Before summer vacation began that year, there was marked uneasiness among the Troy State faculty. Many of them had been called into President Adams's office and questioned about their "loyalty." The two professors who had been Dickey's personal faculty advisers during his two years at Troy had both resigned in protest against the administration's policies. But Dickey himself had had no recent brush with the administration. On May 19 he submitted the required formal request for admission to Troy State for his senior year. On July 18 he received the formal notice granting that request, with instructions to appear for registration at the college on September 11.

Then, on August 12, a Saturday, Dickey received a registered letter from Troy State's dean of men. It said:

This is to advise you that the Student Affairs Committee met to discuss your application for readmission and voted that you not be admitted at this time.

It was pointed out that you deliberately refused to comply with instructions issued by the *Tropolitan*'s faculty adviser and it was agreed that it would be better if you did not enroll at this

institution at this time.
We wish the best for you in all your future endeavors.

The letter was a startling and serious blow: It could mean the end of Dickey's college career. A student who had been refused admission to one state college could not, by Alabama law, be accepted by any other. And though Dickey's record might have won him acceptance by a non-state-endowed school, even with the start of a new academic year less than a month away, he couldn't afford to attend anything but a state-supported institution.

Another problem was that Dickey's $1,800 student loan from the government, which didn't have to be repaid until he finished college, would come due immediately, at a doubled rate of interest, if he remained out of school for six consecutive months. And as his three-month summer vacation was now almost over, he had only three months in which to return to school or find himself faced with a crippling debt.

A member of the *Advertiser* staff learned of Dickey's situation and reported it on Sunday, August 13, in a story headed "TROY STATE TELLS DICKEY NOT TO RETURN THIS FALL."

That same day, determined to find some way out of this unexpected crisis, Dickey conferred with Morris Dees. Dees, a young Montgomery attorney, was a graduate of the University of Alabama and sympathetic to Dr. Rose, its beleaguered president. As an active member of the ACLU, he was also sympathetic to anyone whose constitutional rights he felt were being denied.

Within hours Dees was taking the first steps toward bringing Dickey's case into court. At the same time he sought the moral and financial support of the ACLU on Dickey's behalf, by telephoning a Birmingham attorney who was also active in the organization. (Alabama did not have its own Civil Liberties Union office in Montgomery until 1972.)

"This certainly seems to me like an ACLU case," Dees told Erskine Smith. "It involves the First Amendment rights of freedom of speech and freedom of the press, and rights of academic freedom, as well."

Smith agreed with him.

"I'm willing to handle the case without a fee," Dees said. He asked Smith if the Alabama affiliate of the ACLU could take care of the court costs, which he knew Dickey couldn't pay.

Smith reminded him that the affiliate's budget was small, but promised to bring up the matter before its officers. Soon he reported back that he felt fairly certain the ACLU could provide some financial aid and that it stood in firm support of Dickey's position.

In the meantime, while Dees prepared the necessary documents, the *Advertiser* continued to report Dickey's story to its readers. On Monday it carried an interview with the president of the Troy Student Government Association, who said that he, too, objected to censorship of the *Tropolitan*. "But Dickey was kicked out solely because he disobeyed orders," he added.

Asked if he considered one failure to obey an order sufficient grounds for banning Dickey from the college, the student replied, "People have been kicked out for less."

"DID THE PUNISHMENT FIT THE CRIME?" demanded an *Advertiser* editorial the next day. "Although Congress can under the Constitution make no law abridging the freedom of speech, or of the press," the editorial began, "apparently—as in the Gary Dickey case—Troy State College can and has done so."

That Dickey had been "denied furtherance of his education because he stood up, in a small measure, for one of the freedoms he had fought for in Vietnam" was, the editorial writer declared, "unusually stern punishment.

"That Dickey is justified in his act of disobedience," the editorial concluded, "is underscored by the summation of the student leader: 'People have been kicked out for less.' It can also be said that in certain dictatorships people have been shot for less."

The following day, Wednesday, August 16, a suit was filed in the U.S. District Court for the Middle District of Alabama in the name of Gary Dickey, plaintiff. The defendants named were the Alabama State Board of Education and its officers, including Governor Lurleen Wallace, and Troy State College and its president, Ralph W. Adams.

Dickey was suing for his right to be readmitted to Troy State. His suit made three specific requests.

First, it asked for a hearing, before a district court judge, as to whether or not Dickey had been dismissed from the college without adequate reason.

Second, if the first request was not granted, it asked the judge to order the defendants to grant Dickey a hearing "with advance notice and . . . the rudiments of an adversary proceeding." In this request Dees was making the point that Dickey had been dismissed without any hearing at all—that he had, in other words, been denied the due process of law guaranteed by the Constitution.

Third, if the second request was granted, the suit asked the judge to "retain jurisdiction" in the case until that hearing took place, so that he might review the decision to insure its fairness. As Dees told an *Advertiser* reporter, he did not believe Dickey could get a "fair and impartial hearing in the intellectually deprived atmosphere existing now at Troy State."

At the same time that he was filing Dickey's suit, Dees

was also taking another legal step. Since he knew a crowded court calendar might delay hearing of that suit until the new school year was some months old and Dickey's debt already due, he filed a motion seeking what lawyers call a "preliminary injunction." That is, he asked the district court judge to issue an order to the defendants before a full-scale hearing could take place.

Judge Frank M. Johnson, Jr., responded with all the speed Dickey and Dees could have wished. Two days later, on August 18, he issued the preliminary injunction. It was a ruling that unless Troy State granted Dickey a hearing by August 24 and advised Dickey of its outcome by August 30, his suit would be heard in court on September 1.

The next day, a Saturday, college officials announced that they would decide over the weekend whether to give Dickey a hearing or to prepare, instead, to appear in court to defend his suit against them. And by Tuesday Dickey had been told there would be a hearing at the college on Friday, before the same Student Affairs Committee that had denied him admission less than two weeks earlier.

The hearing was held behind closed doors. Dees told the committee that his client had had a constitutional right to publish the censored editorial. A spokesman for the committee indicated that censorship was not the subject at issue. Dickey was being heard solely "on the charge of insubordination," he said, and had been refused readmission to Troy State simply because he had disobeyed orders. At the close of the hearing the committee members announced that there was no change in their position: Dickey would not be readmitted to Troy State.

A week later, on Monday, September 4—with college registration scarcely a week away—Judge Johnson listened to testimony on the case in his courtroom. President Adams and Dickey were the chief witnesses.

Asked why Dickey's editorial had been censored, President Adams said again that it was because Dickey had criticized the governor and the legislature. An editorial praising them, he explained, could have been published. But because they "owned" the college and the paper, they must not be criticized. "Insubordination" was once more given as the sole reason for refusing Dickey readmission.

Dickey agreed, in his testimony, that he had disobeyed Waites's order, but he added that there was more than a "disciplinary problem" involved—that he had been denied his rights under the Constitution. And Dees, pleading on his behalf, made the same claim of the denial of constitutional rights.

On Friday, September 8, Judge Johnson issued his opinion. It was in Dickey's favor and explained at length the reasoning behind it.

Judge Johnson said he accepted the college's claim that insubordination—the breaking of a rule—had been the "sole basis" of its case against Dickey. And the court recognized, he said, that "certain rules and regulations" were necessary in any educational institution to maintain order and discipline among its students.

However, the judge went on, "school officials have always been bound by the requirement that the rules and regulations *must be reasonable*." President Adams himself, he pointed out, "testified that his general policy of not criticizing the Governor or the State Legislature under any circumstances, regardless of how reasonable or justified the criticism might be, was not for the purpose of maintaining order and discipline among the students," but that the "reason for the rule was that a newspaper could not criticize its owners."

The judge then stated that "the invocation of such a rule" against Dickey was unreasonable. A state cannot force a college student to forfeit his constitutionally protected right of freedom of expression as a condition for his attending a state-supported institution. . . . The attempt to characterize Dickey's conduct . . . as "insubordination" requiring rather severe disciplinary action, does not disguise the basic fact that Dickey was expelled from Troy State College for exercising his constitutionally guaranteed right of academic and/or political expression.

Judge Johnson further stated that

the imposition of intellectual restraints such as the "Adams Rule" . . . violates the basic principles of academic and political expression as guaranteed by our Constitution. . . . Scholarship cannot flourish in an atmosphere of suspicion and distrust. Teachers and students must always remain free to inquire, to study and to evaluate, to gain new maturity and understanding; otherwise our civilization will stagnate and die.

He ordered the defendants in the case to "immediately reinstate" Dickey as a student at Troy State College. They were also told to pay the costs in the case that had been brought against them.

Dickey, however, chose not to return to Troy State. Now that he was eligible to enroll there, he was also eligible to attend another state school. So he finished his college career—and won an award as a journalist—at Alabama's Auburn University, where the "Adams Rule" had never been applied.

8

Lori and the FBI

How would you feel if you learned that the FBI's files held a card with your name on it, marked with the number 100—a code number showing you'd been investigated by the FBI in connection with "subversive matters"? That's what Lori Paton learned when she was a sixteen-year-old high school student in the conservative town of Chester, in northern New Jersey. And that's why Lori, with the help of the ACLU, brought suit against agents of the FBI, the Federal Bureau of Investigation.

Lori's involvement with the FBI began early in 1973, when she was a junior. Although she considered herself a liberal, she was not deeply concerned with politics. However, like most Americans at the time, she was aware that the country was in political turmoil.

The war in Vietnam, then finally coming to an end, had aroused antiwar demonstrations among students and many other groups, and the government's angry reaction to them had left a great deal of bitterness behind. Also, the political scandal known as "Watergate" recently had exploded into the news. It would result within another year in the near-impeachment and resignation of the Republican president, Richard M. Nixon. That scandal had started with a Republican-sponsored cloak-and-dagger break-in of the Democratic party's headquarters in a Washington office complex known as Watergate. The Republican administration then had attempted to cover up the illegal act. Already, Watergate had alerted Americans to the possibility of illegal behavior by some of the highest officials in their government.

Perhaps it was the current Watergate investigation that prompted Lori's choice of an elective social science course that year, in the handsome new high school she was attending in Mendham, Chester's close neighbor. Or perhaps it was simply the lively mind that had already made her an honor student, as well as class secretary and an editor of the school yearbook. The course she chose was new and experimental, designed to introduce students to a wide spectrum of American political opinion. It was called "Left to Right."

Lori and most of her two dozen classmates enjoyed "Left to Right," but some of their parents didn't approve of the course. Those parents—Lori's weren't among them—didn't like the idea that the students were once addressed by an anarchist, and on another occasion by a member of the American Nazi Party.

One day in February the class homework assignment was for each student to write to a specific political party, requesting information about its programs and policies. (The teacher of the course had a list of the political parties of the United States and the addresses of their national headquarters.) The parents of some students refused to let them accept the assignment: They didn't want material from some "radical" party arriving at their home. But Lori wasn't concerned when she learned that the party assigned to her was the "radical" Socialist Labor Party. She wrote her letter, addressed it to the party at 410 West Street, New York, N.Y.—the address she'd brought home with her—and mailed it.

Though she didn't realize it then and never afterward could understand how it had happened, Lori had not used the correct address of the Socialist Labor Party. Instead she had used the address of another party with a very similar name: the Socialist Workers' Party, often referred to as the SWP. According to the FBI, the SWP was a "large" Marxist organization of 1,100 people dedicated to the overthrow of the government. And it was then so high on the FBI's list of subversive organizations that it was under a "mail cover." This was a process that kept the FBI informed about all mail sent to a certain address. In this case the mail cover was on 410 West Street.

Lori's letter therefore took a roundabout way to its destination. First, of course, from her own New Jersey post office it went to the New York City post office that handled mail for the area including 410 West Street. There it landed in the bag of the postman who delivered mail to that neighborhood. But before going out on his route, the postman obeyed an order that had come down to him some time before: He took out the letters for 410 West Street and handed them over to a postal inspector who had his own orders. The inspector made a list for the FBI of the senders of all those letters. Then he returned the letters to the postman for delivery.

No one seemed to notice that the name on Lori's envelope was the Socialist Labor Party, not the SWP. Or, if anyone did notice, it may have been assumed that the sender had made what was perhaps a common error. The result was that the New York office of the FBI was informed that Lori Paton, who lived on Mile Drive in Chester, New Jersey, had made "contacts with the national office, SWP, 410 West Street, NYC."

That information appeared in a memorandum from the FBI's New York office to its office in Newark, New Jersey. When no information about Lori could be found in Newark's files, Special Agent John Devlin was sent to Chester to "contact sources and conduct criminal investigation regarding Lori Paton, Mile Drive, to determine if she is involved in subversive activity."

Devlin consulted the local directory when he reached Chester. The only Paton he found there, an Arthur H. Paton—Lori's father—also lived on Mile Drive. So Devlin checked that name with the local credit bureau. There he learned no more than the names of Paton's wife and his respectable employer, and that Mr. and Mrs. Paton had lived in Chester for several years. The Patons' credit rating was apparently excellent.

Next Devlin visited the Chester chief of police, and there, too, he found no information of the kind he was seeking. Chief Edward Strait said there had never been any trouble with the Patons—except once, he added conscientiously, when the Paton dog had managed to slip free of its leash and wander off by himself.

Devlin's third visit was to Mendham High School. Now,

at this point, it's necessary to explain that there are a couple of unanswered questions in the story of Lori and the FBI.

The first question has to do with how the New York FBI office learned where Lori lived. Asked about it later, under oath, Lori said she didn't think she had put her own name and address on the outside of her letter's envelope. If she was right, her name and address could have been learned only by opening the envelope and looking at the letter itself. But the FBI claimed that "mail cover" inspectors never opened envelopes, because that would be illegal. The question of how the FBI found Lori's name and address could therefore never be answered satisfactorily.

The second question had to do with Devlin's visit to Mendham High School. In his testimony, Devlin stated that Police Chief Strait had told him the Patons had a daughter who had attended that school. But the chief himself testified that he couldn't have told Devlin that. If he had mentioned anything about Arthur Paton's daughter and her school, he would certainly have said that she went to school in Chester. He wouldn't have known, he said, that she was among the small group of Chester students sent to the new high school in Mendham.

There's no doubt, however, that Devlin did go to Lori's school, asked for the principal, Richard Matthews, and talked with him and his assistant. After identifying himself as an FBI agent, Devlin told the two men that he was investigating someone who was probably a graduate of Mendham High School. Matthews explained to him that the school was so new it had had only one graduating class so far, the previous year. Devlin then mentioned Lori's name, and both the principal and his assistant smiled. Matthews, assuming that Devlin must be mistaken about the name of the person he was inquiring about, said the only Lori Paton they knew was still a student.

Devlin, apparently surprised, said he nevertheless wanted information about Lori. She was, he said, "in contact with an organization that the FBI is interested in investigating."

Matthews then realized that Lori could have had "contact" with such an organization as part of her work for the "Left to Right" course. So he described the course briefly and offered to send for someone who could furnish Devlin with more information about it—William Gabrielson, head of the school's social science program.

At that point Devlin ended the interview abruptly. Testifying about it later, Matthews said that Devlin had left "after saying something like 'Well, I think we will just drop it and leave it at that.'"

Matthews himself, however, wasn't ready to drop it. He called Gabrielson to his office and told him about the FBI agent's visit. Gabrielson, Matthews recalled afterward, "couldn't believe that that had happened, and he was concerned." Matthews was concerned, too.

Before school closed that day, Gabrielson, along with the teacher of Lori's course, called Lori out of her final-period class and spoke to her in the hall. They didn't mention the SWP. Like Lori herself and everyone else who learned of the FBI's visit during the next several weeks, they believed Lori's letter had reached its intended destination, the Socialist Labor Party.

Recalling that conversation during her own testimony, Lori said, "Before they said anything else, they told me not to be upset and not to be worried, and then they only told me, I suppose, what they knew. They didn't want to alarm me that an agent had been there checking into my activities."

Gabrielson then asked Lori to tell her parents about the agent's visit. He said he himself hoped to make public what he called "an offensive action," so that "it wouldn't happen again."

That same day Gabrielson got in touch with a television station and with the offices of his congressman and a New Jersey assemblywoman, Ann Klein. The television station showed no interest. The congressman's office advised him to put his complaint into a letter. Ann Klein's office called back to suggest that Gabrielson telephone Stephen Nagler, executive director of the ACLU of New Jersey. Nagler was definitely interested. He wanted a letter spelling out exactly what had happened.

By the next day, Mendham High was swept by the news that an FBI agent had visited the school. "FBI INVESTIGATES AT MHS" read a headline in the school's one-page mimeographed newspaper. The story didn't mention Lori's name and the writer, of course, didn't know Lori had used a wrong address.

According to the story, the agent had inquired about a letter "written by a Mendham student to the Socialist Labor Party in New York City," the principal had explained it "was associated with a course called 'Left to Right,'" and "the agent was satisfied and left." But the third and final paragraph of the story demanded editorially, "How did the FBI obtain this information? Did they read the letter? . . . Is this not an infringement on the rights of the individual to obtain information? What will come next? Is this Mendham's equivalent to Watergate?"

Lori's fellow students soon learned who had been the object of the FBI's inquiries. With her permission, Gabrielson discussed those inquiries in his classes. There were discussions of them in other classes, too, in and out of Lori's presence. One math teacher made it clear to his students that he felt Lori should never have allowed the investigation to become known publicly.

Remarks were also made to Lori in the halls—some good-natured, some that hurt her whether they were meant to or not. Over and over a school wit would come up behind her, thrust a finger into her back as if it were a gun, and bark, "FBI! Get your hands up!"

Lori suddenly had become "famous"—"in more of a criminal sense, not a good sense," she put it once. Some days she left school early just to escape from her new and unwelcome notoriety.

Her first reaction to the news of the FBI's investigation had been simple anger over something done behind her back. It seemed to her the FBI agent should have come to her directly if he wanted to know why she had written that letter.

But gradually her feelings grew more complicated. For one thing, she came to understand and agree with the deep resentment Gabrielson and the school principal felt toward the FBI. The two men were dedicated to giving students the widest possible range of educational experience. That was the purpose of such courses as "Left to Right." They thought inquiries like Devlin's could intimidate students in the future—make them fearful even of asking questions about unpopular but perfectly lawful political groups. And, if that happened, the school's effectiveness and the students' education would be seriously hampered.

Lori became distressed for her parents, too. The Patons had mentioned to neighbors that Gabrielson wanted to publicize what had happened to Lori and that since Lori agreed to it they supported her firmly. But the neighbors shared the math teacher's disapproval. The FBI had done nothing wrong, they had told the Patons, adding that the wisest thing would have been to hush up the whole matter immediately.

Lori also began to worry about her future, once it occurred to her that her name might be in the FBI's permanent files. Couldn't that affect a college's decision about whether or not to accept her? And what about the job in the Far East she hoped to have some day with the State Department? Would the government hire anybody the FBI kept a record on?

Then a friend of Lori's father pointed out that even if Lori changed her mind about her career and wanted to make her way in the business world instead, she could still face problems. "They check you out, and the slightest thing on a record could mar you," the friend said, speaking of employers to whom Lori might apply for any position of trust. "No one would say anything to you, such as 'Eighteen years ago you were investigated in high school,'" he explained. "You just simply would not get the job."

Lori admitted later that she had become greatly disturbed. She felt, she said, "as if in some ways my life had been taken out of my hands."

Gabrielson's letter to Stephen Nagler of New Jersey's ACLU brought a clear response. If there were no objections on the part of Lori or her parents, Nagler said—and there were no such objections—a letter would be sent to the FBI office in Newark. It would ask certain questions about Devlin's investigation of Lori and state that unless satisfactory answers to those questions were received, "further action" would be taken.

The letter Nagler referred to went out from the office of the organization's counsel, Frank Askin. Askin, a former newspaperman, was also a member of the ACLU's National Board of Directors, a professor at the Rutgers University School of Law, and director of the school's Constitutional Litigation Clinic. He and the young student "interns" staffing the clinic did a great deal of volunteer work for the ACLU of New Jersey. They helped make it possible for that organization to deal with many more cases every year than its own small paid staff could possibly handle.

The letter Askin sent, dated June 13, 1973, was addressed to J. Wallace LaPrade, the special agent in charge of the FBI office in Newark. Copies went to Washington, D.C., to the acting director of the FBI and to the attorney general of the United States. In the letter Askin explained how Lori's letter had come to be written, describing it as having been sent to the Socialist Labor Party since that's where Lori still believed it had gone. He also described Devlin's visit to Mendham High School.

Then Askin asked LaPrade how the FBI had learned of Lori's letter. Next he wanted to know if everyone who wrote to the Socialist Labor Party was investigated and, if not, why Lori had been singled out. And, finally, he asked "what records or notations have been made in the Bureau's files" about Lori or anyone else at Mendham High School.

Late in June, before Askin had gotten a reply from LaPrade, he sent one of his young clinic interns to Chester to ask Lori for any material she had received in response to her letter. The Mendham school had already closed for the year, but Lori and the law student were admitted to the building. Together they searched through pamphlets and other items the members of the "Left to Right" class had obtained through the mail.

What she had received, Lori told the intern, had been disappointing. She described it as mostly anti-Democratic and anti-Republican propaganda, so uninteresting that she had paid little attention to it. One thing she did recall was that it had arrived in two manila envelopes.

Neither those envelopes nor their contents could be found. Lori concluded that they had been taken home by students who wanted souvenirs of the "Left to Right" class.

The intern then questioned Lori about the address from

which those envelopes had been sent, and Lori said she thought it had been somewhere on a Charles Lane in New York. To learn the telephone number of the Socialist Labor Party office at that address, the intern dialed telephone information. He was told that no office of that party was located on Charles Lane. "But there's a listing for the Young Alliance of the Socialist Workers' Party at that address," the operator added.

And that was how Lori and her friends and the ACLU finally learned that she had never been in touch with the party she believed she had written to. Presumably her letter had gone first to the Socialist Workers' Party—the SWP—at 410 West Street and then to its Charles Lane youth branch.

Some days later, early in July, Askin received a reply to his own letter. Special Agent LaPrade, in charge of the Newark FBI office, had written:

After carefully reviewing the facts in this matter, I have concluded there was no impropriety on the part of investigative personnel of this Bureau and that the FBI has no knowledge of any letter Ms. Paton may have sent to the Socialist Labor Party. You may be assured that Ms. Paton is not the subject of an investigation by this Bureau and that the FBI does not maintain a general policy of surveillance of correspondence of political groups such as the Socialist Labor Party.

Askin, reading the letter with his new knowledge of where Lori's letter had actually gone, felt LaPrade had raised more questions than he had answered. If the FBI had seen Lori's letter, then it knew she had sent it to the address of the Socialist Workers' Party. In that case the FBI might be saying, truthfully, that it had no knowledge of "any letter Ms. Paton may have sent to the Socialist Labor Party."

But if the FBI meant to claim that it had "no knowledge" at all of Lori's letter, then why had a man identifying himself as an FBI agent gone to Chester to investigate Lori? Could the man have been an imposter—someone pretending to represent the FBI? That possibility seemed highly unlikely. Therefore, presuming that Lori had been investigated by a legitimate FBI agent, how could the FBI now claim that she was "not the subject of an investigation by this Bureau"?

Askin conferred with Stephen Nagler at the Newark ACLU office. They were convinced that Lori's letter had been intercepted by the FBI. They believed such interception was a violation of a citizen's right, according to both the Constitution and a federal statute that forbids obstructing the mail or opening anyone's mail in order to "pry into his business."

Nagler said he felt sure that what had happened to Lori had happened to many other young people. "We hear that a lot of that kind of thing goes on," he said, "but school officials handle it as part of routine business. In this case we had a school principal who was a little more sensitive."

Askin, an expert on constitutional law, remembered that the great Supreme Court Justice Oliver Wendell Holmes had once written, "The United States may give up the Post Office when it sees fit, but while it carries it on, the use of the mails is almost as much a part of free speech as the the right to use our tongues." Askin and Nagler were in accord about Lori's case. They wanted to pursue it.

Gabrielson, the social science department head, was consulted. More important, so were Lori and her parents. All agreed that the letter from LaPrade should not be allowed to end the matter. So, late in July, the ACLU of New Jersey made an announcement to the press. It said a suit was being brought, on Lori's behalf, in the Federal District Court in Newark against "J. Wallace LaPrade et al."—that is, against LaPrade and other agents of the FBI.

Suddenly, overnight, Lori's name was being read and heard all over the country. Pictures showed her slender face, framed by her long straight-hanging hair, looking steadily into the camera. Next to a front-page story on the latest revelations of the Watergate cover-up and President Nixon's efforts to prove he had not been involved in it, a *New York Times* headline read "JERSEY GIRL SUES FBI OVER INTERCEPTED LETTER." Askin intended to prove that in the case of Lori Paton the FBI was attempting a cover-up of its own.

The suit being brought in Lori's name asked the court to order the FBI to destroy any records it had in its files about her. It also asked for damages—$15,000 as compensation for the embarrassment and humiliation Lori had suffered and $50,000 in punitive damages. And it asked the court to forbid the FBI's further investigation or interference with any mail sent to any lawful political organization. In this third section of the suit, a class action, Lori would be representing the entire "class" of people whose mail might be treated as hers had been.

Neither Askin nor the Patons regarded the actual money they demanded as important in itself. Askin, in fact, advised Lori not to expect any substantial sum. His reason for demanding monetary damages was a legal one. He felt that it would improve Lori's chances of having her suit heard before a judge and a jury, rather than a judge alone. A judge unsympathetic to her case could simply dismiss it.

Announcement of the suit brought a sharp reaction from some of the same people who had always said Lori should have kept quiet about the FBI's investigation from the start. She shouldn't have "rocked the boat," as they put it. Now they were saying "So that's it! She's been doing it for the money all along!"

Furthermore, two men, unnamed and described only as

"very familiar with FBI procedures," gave an interview to the local daily newspaper in which they suggested that Lori had probably done something more than write an innocent letter. The FBI, they said, would scarcely have "bothered with a 16-year-old high school girl unless she were involved in something else."

Lori wasn't going to have an easy time of it. But she felt more and more certain that what she was doing was right. She was further convinced of it when she learned that the next "Left to Right" class was only about half the size hers had been. It seemed all too likely that students were now avoiding that course for fear that they, too, might become targets of an FBI investigation.

By early winter Lori was traveling to Newark to give sworn testimony before a notary public, while a stenographer took down every word. Such pretrial discovery proceedings give both sides in a lawsuit the opportunity to learn about each other's case before the trial in a courtroom takes place. Askin asked her questions. So did the lawyer from the U.S. Department of Justice who represented the FBI.

One of the first questions the FBI lawyer asked her was "Do you believe that you were deprived of your constitutional rights?"

"I certainly do," Lori replied firmly.

While the testimony of Lori and others was being taken in preparation for a trial, Askin also was trying to subpoena documents from the FBI files. He was having little success. The FBI insisted that some of the papers Askin hoped to see couldn't be released for reasons of "national security."

Askin was running into another snag, too. The FBI's lawyer wouldn't permit Special Agent Devlin to answer Askin's questions about the FBI's use of mail covers. Askin argued that the "entire practice of mail surveillance is relevant to this case and we should be able to pursue it." The FBI's lawyer flatly disagreed.

Some weeks later, in January 1974, Lori's case received another setback. Federal District Court Judge James A. Coolahan dismissed the class action part of her suit. He ruled that he could not recognize her as representing, in the words Askin had used, "all persons who have been or will become engaged in correspondence with dissident political groups."

Lori wasn't typical of that "class," the judge said, because—as the FBI admitted—she had had only "mild contact" with the SWP as a result of her letter. Other people's letters, however, might lead to the uncovering of "illegal or suspicious activities."

Spring arrived, and then summer. Lori was graduated from high school and was accepted by the University of Virginia. One late August day, when she was out shopping—she would be leaving for college within the week— her mother received a call from Askin's office. The judge had issued his opinion on the two remaining parts of Lori's suit.

Since the FBI's investigation of her had proved that Lori was innocent of any involvement with the SWP, he declared that the investigation had done her reputation no harm. "No one doubts," Judge Coolahan had written,

that there has not been even the smallest degree of impropriety, legal or otherwise, in her communication with the SWP. The FBI has placed into the public record its file showing that there was not one shred of evidence obtained through the Paton investigation. The opinion of this court reiterating the innocence of Lori Paton, now becomes part of the public record.

The judge had continued:

As she has failed to show injury to her reputation, plaintiff has also failed to show other injury. Her privacy has not been invaded. None of her own time was taken up in the investigation. She was not harassed in any way. Her right of political inquiry has not been abridged; information requested from the SWP was received.

With those words the judge was, in effect, invalidating Lori's claim for personal damages because he agreed with the FBI's contention that she had not suffered in any way from the investigation. He also was invalidating her claim for punitive damages because he further agreed with the FBI that it had done nothing illegal or unconstitutional in using a mail cover.

The judge did disagree with the FBI on one point, however. He had decided the FBI did not, as it insisted, have the legal right to keep the record of Lori's investigation in its files. "Insofar as plaintiff Paton's files contain no information which could be useful to the FBI in the exercise of its law enforcement functions," he had written, "and the existence of these records may at a later time become a detriment to her, this Court holds that the Paton file should be removed from the custody of the Government and destroyed."

Lori's future, it appeared, was once more in her own hands. And the judge's order to destroy her record was widely hailed in the press as the "first of its kind."

But the judge's order was not, in fact, the first one requiring the FBI to destroy—to expunge—the record it was holding on an admittedly innocent young person. An order to expunge had been issued just a few months earlier on behalf of Dale Menard, whose case deserves a brief mention here.

On the evening of August 9, 1965, when Menard was a nineteen-year-old student in California, he fell asleep on a

Los Angeles park bench while waiting for a friend. A Los Angeles policeman, finding a wallet on the ground near the bench, awakened Menard and took him to the local police station because he suspected Menard had stolen the wallet.

Menard was held at the station for two days, until the police were convinced he had committed no crime. Then, without having been formally charged, he was released. But during those two days the police had sent his fingerprints, along with a report of his detention, to the FBI headquarters in Washington for its criminal files.

Menard requested the expungement of the FBI record, and his request was refused. With the help of the ACLU, he then brought suit in a case that seesawed back and forth between district and appeals courts for ten years. When the expungement of his record was finally won, the victory established an important precedent: It was illegal for the FBI to keep the record of an innocent person in its criminal files.

Of course, Lori and Askin could find some satisfaction in having won the expungement of her FBI record in far less time—in under two years. But Lori's victory was hers alone. It had established no precedent. In her case the district judge had not ruled that it was illegal for the FBI to use a mail cover on a political party, or to carry out the kind of investigation it had made of Lori, or to keep an admittedly innocent person's name in its "subversive matters" files, which are separate from its criminal files.

"As things stand now," Askin said, "the FBI is free to go on conducting these investigations, and if someone is lucky enough to catch them at it then that someone can have his record destroyed. But what about the people who don't find out about it?"

A *New York Times* editorial pointed out that this could

"stigmatize innocent persons for life, without ever affording them the opportunity to clear themselves of totally unwarranted suspicions."

Lori also felt the fight that had been started in her name was unfinished. So, with her parents' support, she and Askin decided to appeal the judge's decision that denied her damages and allowed the FBI to continue its practice of instituting mail covers on lawful political organizations.

The FBI, for its part, wasn't entirely happy with the district court's decision, either. Believing it had a legal right to keep the record of Lori's investigation in its file, it appealed the part of the decision that ordered the record expunged.

The next chapter in the history of Lori's case began to unfold nearly a year later in Philadelphia, where the U.S. Court of Appeals for the Third District sits. There, in June 1975, the lawyers for both sides appeared before the court. After presenting their arguments, all they could do was await the court's decision.

The whole summer passed. In the meantime, Congress had begun to investigate the handling of citizens' records by government agencies. One of the investigating committees already had heard testimony from Askin, because he was an expert on constitutional law and the lawyer involved in Lori's case.

Early in the fall of 1975, Askin was invited to appear in Washington again, and this time Lori was asked to testify, too. Earlier Lori had refused to be interviewed on television. She already had been the subject of a good many news reports. "I don't want to be a media freak," she had explained to Askin then.

But Lori had learned that publicity could be useful in defense of a cause, and late in October she, too, went to Washington with a statement to read before a congressional committee. In it she described her "disillusionment with the government's conduct." She also reported that the U.S. Court of Appeals had just—on October 14— reached a decision on her case that offered hope for the future.

The decision, with its numerous citations of legal precedents, filled sixteen printed pages, but its conclusion can be stated fairly briefly. The appeals court had ruled that the lower district court should not have decided Lori's case without a fuller exploration of the many factual or legal contentions made by both sides. And it sent the case back to the district court "for further proceedings consistent with this opinion." The case of *Paton* v. *LaPrade* was thus back in Newark, in the same court in which it had begun.

Askin immediately submitted requests for the FBI documents and records he had not before been able to obtain. The FBI still refused to supply them, on the grounds of possible damage to national security. Askin asked the judge to give an order for their release. He waited—and waited and waited—for the order to be issued.

But, at the same time, certain events were occurring that had some bearing on Lori's case. In April 1976, a Senate committee issued a far-reaching and sharply worded report about the FBI and other domestic intelligence agencies it had been studying for over a year. The report rebuked the FBI for "investigating far too many people, often for the wrong reasons or none at all." It said the FBI had employed "illegal and questionable" techniques, such as mail opening.

The committee's conclusion was that "the natural tendency of government is toward abuse of power." The "wise restraints" of the constitutional system, it said, "guard against this tendency," but it added that "in the field of intelligence, those restraints have too often been ignored." The committee said that "a fundamental reform" of the domestic intelligence service was urgently needed, and it called for new laws to carry it out.

In August 1976, the FBI, finally ordered to do so by Judge Coolahan, made four documents available to Askin. They were helpful, but Askin knew the FBI was withholding still others that had a bearing on the case. He persisted in his demands for more material, and the FBI persisted in its refusal to supply it. The bureau was *stonewalling,* to use the word made famous during the congressional investigation of the Watergate affair, when the Nixon White House consistently delayed producing material Congress sought. And Judge Coolahan showed little enthusiasm for ordering the FBI to abandon the practice.

Finally, in January 1978—Lori was twenty-one years old by then—the chief judge of the district court, Lawrence A. Whipple, removed Judge Coolahan from the Paton case and took it over himself. Chief Judge Whipple then ordered the FBI to turn over to Askin the material he had been demanding for years. Some of it Askin described as "startling." The documents made clear, for example, that during one period in 1973 the FBI had opened "subversive" records on New Jersey residents at the rate of two a day. There must have been, Askin commented, "an awful lot of dangerous folk running around New Jersey in 1973."

More important to Lori's case, Askin found in the newly received material a memorandum explaining just why the FBI had been so interested in the SWP. According to the memorandum, the FBI's investigation of the party had nothing to do with the "national security" the FBI claimed to be protecting. Instead, the investigation of the SWP had been made because its members were active protestors against America's participation in the war in Vietnam. Such protestors were regarded as enemies by the Nixon administration. The mail cover had thus been instituted to identify new SWP members and sympathizers, who might later qualify for the administration's "enemy list."

"What the FBI was engaged in," Askin wrote afterward, "was not legitimate law-enforcement activity at all. Rather it was operating as a political police force opposing and harassing the political opponents of the government in power."

Less than a year after he had assumed responsibility for the case, Chief Judge Whipple handed down his decision. He ruled that the practice of using mail covers on organizations regarded as "subversive" or "national security risks" was unconstitutional.

"National security is too ambiguous and broad a term," his decision stated.

. . . Invalidating a regulation on its face is strong medicine. Nevertheless it is the only cure. National security as a basis for a mail cover is unconstitutionally vague . . . an investigation can be initiated on the assertions of an overzealous public official who disagrees with the unorthodox, yet constitutionally protected political views of a group or person. It allows officials to pursue their predilections.

The FBI and the Postal Service immediately let it be known that they regarded the judge's ruling as effective only in New Jersey.

Judge Whipple didn't mince words when he called representatives of both to his courtroom. He reminded them that he was a federal judge, not a New Jersey judge, and that his ruling was valid throughout the nation. If they wished to challenge his decision, he added, they were of course free to do so in the court of appeals. But until his ruling was reversed, he told them, they would be held in contempt of court if they began any new "national security" mail covers anywhere in the United States.

This time there was no question that the victory of Lori

Paton, plaintiff, was complete. Her FBI record was ordered expunged. The court had established that her constitutional rights had been violated, and that the violation of those rights entitled her to damages. The FBI's offer of damages was only a single dollar, but the amount was accepted as satisfactory. An award of many thousands could not have vindicated Lori more thoroughly. Finally, Judge Whipple ordered the FBI to pay court costs—that is, the expenses incurred in fighting Lori's case through the courts.

Lori's court testimony became one of the sources of information used by Congress when, shortly afterward, it drew up and passed a new Federal Privacy Act. One portion of the act forbids the FBI, in Askin's words, to collect and maintain "records describing how people exercise their rights of free speech and association under the First Amendment of the Constitution."

Lori Paton had learned the importance of the First Amendment. She also had learned something about a citizen's responsibility to defend—if necessary, at the cost of considerable time and effort—the "rights of free speech and association" regarded as so vital by the framers of the Constitution.

9

Hard Times and the Granville Board of Education

In testifying during a legal action against the board of education of New York's Granville Central School District, one of the four plaintiffs, high school student Richard Williams, was asked why he had wanted to publish a newspaper.

"Well," Richard said, "for entertainment for the students, and Granville is not very exciting, there is nothing to do at all, so I decided it would be good for everybody just to have a laugh and just for entertainment."

How well the four students involved in the venture succeeded is made very clear in Judge James T. Foley's decision on the case. That United States district court judge
wrote:

If the winter was becoming too dull in Granville, the distribution
and sale of this newspaper, with its complete sexual format and
content, on the streets and places near the high school, to its
students, changed all that and stirred the small village from any
winter slumber it may have been in.

Later on in his decision Judge Foley also said, "It is hard
for my mind to accept with equanimity the proposition that
this high school adventure, similar to the expected high
school pranks that often occur, rises to the stature of a
federal constitutional case."

Certainly the four students who started the unofficial
newspaper didn't expect to become participants in a lawsuit. But the publication in question not only shook up a
fair share of Granville's 3,000 residents; it started a legal
battle about free speech and other civil rights that went to
the Supreme Court before the action ended in 1980.

The events leading up to the legal action began in November or December of 1978, when John Tiedeman, a
junior in the high school, conceived the idea of starting a
publication. He discussed it with Donna Thomas, a senior,
who reacted enthusiastically. Such a project, they agreed,
would give them something constructive to do during the
winter and give them a taste of the journalistic life, as well.

What they wanted, Donna and John agreed, was something lively, something that would poke fun at teachers
and other students, that would satirize life in school, and
that would entertain and perhaps startle its readers. They
decided to pattern their publication after the *National
Lampoon,* a magazine described by Judge Foley, with ju-

dicial reserve, as ". . . a monthly magazine of national circulation, the content of which is heavily weighted toward spoofs of sexual behavior."

Donna and John enlisted the help of Richard Williams and David Jones, two students who some time before had created a cartoon character named "Jock." Then they all set to work on the newspaper they decided to call *Hard Times*.

Lunch hours gave them the chance to confer and to ask classmates for article suggestions and jokes. Each of the four worked at home on the assignments they parceled out to one another. At the close of the school day they would gather in the room of history teacher George Mager, who, like other Granville high school teachers, stayed after school each day to talk to students who might need help or guidance. It was in Mager's room that the finished articles were edited and sometimes rewritten or discarded.

At first Mager didn't know what the four students were working on. But, after a few days, intrigued by the laughter and giggles from the group, he asked them what they were doing.

They showed him their work. Mager read the completed articles and suggested that he correct the grammar and punctuation. "If you're going to do it," he said, "do it right."

For several weeks thereafter, Mager saw the articles and cartoons as they were finished. He suggested changes in grammar and in writing style. And, when he saw the general direction the newspaper was taking—following the *National Lampoon* in irreverence and freedom of expression—he suggested that certain of the articles be forgotten. There was no question of censorship on Mager's part. He was acting as the friend the students considered him, suggesting that certain articles might cause trouble for them. They accepted some of his recommendations but not all. They decided, for example, not to give up their lead editorial, entitled "A Close-up on Masturbation."

Mager allowed the four writer-editor-cartoonists to store their completed material in a closet in his classroom, and said he would allow the printed magazine to be stored there, too. Actually he wasn't at all sure the students would ever complete the task they had set for themselves. Some of John Tiedeman's earlier ideas hadn't survived, and Mager had seen more than one student's enthusiasm evaporate in the heat of hard work.

But these four persevered. The number of impudent pieces piled up on the closet shelf. The style was amateurish. The writing lacked the bite and wit of the *National Lampoon* but none of its disregard for conventional language and subject matter.

One article about the school lunchroom said, among other things, "The school policy is, if it won't crawl off the plate, it's okay to serve." And "Mystery meat used in superburgers, and hot beef sandwiches is not your average farm raised livestock but more likely some poor pet that got too close to the kitchen. . . . So remember the next time you munch down on a superburger, it might just be your long-lost pet."

Another article, entitled "K. M. Report," discussed the New Year activities of "one of our local ladies of the evening." There was a short bit of writing called "Watch Out for the Wrestling Cheerleaders," which appeared to evaluate several girl students for qualities other than cheerleading.

After reading these and other pieces of copy for *Hard Times*, Mager made another suggestion to its creators. He advised them to sell the magazine off the school grounds and to make it clear that the publication had no connection with the school itself.

Sometime in mid-January, Mager asked Frederick Reed, the school's assistant principal, if he had heard any rumors about the forthcoming appearance of a student publication. When Reed said he hadn't, Mager told him that one was in the making and gave him the names of the students who were working on *Hard Times*. But Mager said nothing about the kind of articles and cartoons he had read and seen.

Reed then summoned John Tiedeman to his office. According to their court testimony, both agreed that Reed had said he was not concerned with what students did away from the school. Both agreed that Reed had neither asked to see the newspaper nor questioned John about what it contained. Both agreed that Reed made no attempt to forbid publication. Both agreed that Reed had talked about the pain that some forms of humor could cause people and that the use of names might provoke embarrassment and anger. And both agreed that Reed had mentioned a previous student publication that had resulted in the suspension of its creators and that Reed had said he did not want John to get into trouble.

John's and Reed's testimony differed, however, in their understanding of Reed's motive in calling the meeting. Reed later stated that he was trying to warn John against publishing anything. Like many public school administrators, Reed believed that a school newspaper or magazine was an invitation to trouble. He expected parents and the school board to hold the school responsible for its contents, in spite of the various court decisions limiting administrative control over student publications.

John, on the other hand, assumed that Reed was giving him advice on how to publish the paper without running the risk of punishment. And he and his coworkers took that advice and made changes in the newspaper. They eliminated real names to avoid giving offense, and altered the cover layout to include a headline that ran diagonally across the page. Large letters proclaimed the publication "UNCENSORED—VULGAR—IMMORAL!!!" And two lines at the bottom of the page announced that "WE ARE NOT RESPONSIBLE FOR ANY ISSUES FOUND ON SCHOOL PROPERTY." With such admonitions prominently displayed, the student publishers felt they had put sufficient distance between *Hard Times* and Granville High School.

During the week after John's meeting with Reed, the revision was completed and the entire publication neatly typed for photocopying. Some of the typing was done in the school typing room after school. (Such after-school use of typewriters was an established practice.) Some of the typing, however, was done off school property. A friend of Donna's who had access to a photocopying machine reproduced and stapled the pages.

The first edition of *Hard Times*, about ninety copies, was brought to school Wednesday, January 24, and stored in Mager's closet. After school that day the publishers took about seventy copies to Stewart's, a nearby grocery and candy store, where they sold them for 25 cents each, doing their best to restrict sales to senior high school students or adults. They sold sixteen dollars' worth of *Hard Times* and spent the proceeds on dinner at a local restaurant.

That afternoon a copy of the newspaper "surfaced," as Judge Foley put it, in the school. It was taken from a ninth-grade student by a teacher who then delivered it to the high school principal, William Butler. Butler read the publication. It was, to quote Richard Emery, the New York Civil Liberties attorney for the four students in their subsequent lawsuit,

a sophomoric spoof on Granville school life. Its emphasis is sexual humor. Of 17 short features, 12 in some way allude to sex and eight dwell on it. None contain so-called four-letter words, but several could be considered offensive if the reader did not think they were funny or, at least, silly.

Dr. Butler didn't consider the newspaper either funny or silly. He showed it to Assistant Principal Reed, who realized that this was the publication he had discussed in rather vague terms with John Tiedeman. Dr. Butler also got in touch with District Principal D. L. Miller to tell him about it.

None of the school officials knew where *Hard Times* had been produced, but they decided to keep a close watch on the school's photocopying machine to make sure it wasn't used to turn out additional copies. This was the only action they decided to take at that time.

The school administrators might have continued this policy of watchful waiting indefinitely. But something happened to prod them into taking more vigorous action.

The day after *Hard Times* made its appearance, Mrs. Beverly Tatko, president of the local board of education, was told by her high school–student son about the kind of newspaper that John Tiedeman and his friends had produced. He also told her that Mr. Mager had "edited" the paper and that it had been stored in his classroom.

Mrs. Tatko asked her son to buy a copy, which he did the next day. Over the weekend Mrs. Tatko and her husband read and discussed the newspaper, which they agreed was the "worst and filthiest" publication they had ever seen.

On Monday Miller and Butler had another short discussion about *Hard Times*. Inasmuch as nothing had yet disturbed the peace of Granville, they decided to continue their policy of watchful waiting.

Then Mrs. Tatko appeared in Miller's office with her copy of *Hard Times*. She wanted to know what the district principal intended to do about the students who had produced the newspaper and about Mr. Mager, who, according to her son, had edited it.

Miller summoned Butler, and the two men explained to Mrs. Tatko that they didn't yet know the degree of school involvement in the project and that they were proceeding cautiously until more facts emerged. Mrs. Tatko said that if Miller and Butler were not as upset by the newspaper as she was, she would call a special meeting of the board of education to discuss it. She thought the students should be punished and that Mager should explain his part in the undertaking. She planned, she said, to get a copy of *Hard Times* for each member of the board before the meeting was convened.

Miller later testified that it was his own decision to call board of education meetings for the coming Tuesday and Wednesday. But Judge Foley recognized the stimulating effect Mrs. Tatko's visit had had. He wrote, "It is a fair assessment of the facts to conclude that the investigatory efforts of Dr. Butler and Mr. Miller became more intensive following the meeting with Mrs. Tatko."

These efforts began as soon as Mrs. Tatko left Miller's office Monday morning. Butler questioned Mager as to how much he had known about the newspaper during its preparation and to what extent he had helped produce it. The teacher admitted to correcting grammar and offering a storage place. When Butler left Mager's room, he took with him the remaining copies of *Hard Times*, as well as the master copy from which the others had been reproduced.

Next, Butler and Miller interviewed the four originators of the newspaper, the three boys at one time and Donna later. All unhesitatingly described the project and their involvement in it, and named students who had been involved to a lesser degree. (These students were interviewed the next day and eventually exempted from any disciplinary action.)

Miller and Butler then scheduled a meeting of the school board for the following evening, Tuesday, January 30. They invited the parents of the originators of *Hard Times* to attend.

By Tuesday morning rumors were flying up and down the school corridors about what was going to happen to the newspaper's staff. The staff's reaction was a mixture of apprehension, perplexity, and some indignation. It was clear to them that they were in trouble, but not at all clear why they should be. Reed and Mager had known about *Hard Times* before it appeared and had made no effort to stop publication. Furthermore, the magazine had been produced only partially on and with the aid of school property, and it had not been sold on school grounds.

Later on Tuesday, seven or eight of the newspaper's contributors—Donna was not available—went to see Butler to find out exactly what was in store for them. Butler told them that no one knew what would be done—that a decision about punishment probably would be made at the board of education meeting that evening. He did say that the judgment would be made "on the fact that you have corrected it, edited it, typed, stored it, et cetera, on school property."

According to Butler's testimony, his talk with the students moved from the particulars of the case to a general discussion of discipline and suspension. Then he suggested that if the people of Granville disapproved of *Hard Times* and believed it to be connected with the school, they "might have a grudge against the school" and "strike out" against it by voting down the next school budget.

When the students didn't seem to understand his reasoning, Butler went over the ground again. And when they seemed to have missed the point a second time, he dropped the subject of the budget.

The meeting with Butler did nothing to reassure the four originators of *Hard Times*. In fact, they were convinced that they were going to be punished and, in their view, unfairly punished. Feeling that they should do something, but not knowing what, they talked to Mager about the situation. He suggested that they get in touch with the New York Civil Liberties Union. He thought that organization might be willing to defend them against the school administration, should a defense prove necessary.

A phone call by the students to the Albany office of the NYCLU was received sympathetically. But, since the Albany staff works primarily to advance the cause of civil rights by lobbying the New York State legislature, Richard B. Wolf, the attorney there, referred their appeal to the New York City office.

There it was quickly decided that punishment of the students would violate the First Amendment right of free speech and make a good case for the NYCLU to defend. Also, it would give the civil liberties organization a chance to test in the courts its belief that students had the right of free speech on school grounds as well as off them. Wolf, of the Albany office, and Richard Emery were assigned to follow the situation.

At the Tuesday evening meeting of the Granville Board of Education, the question of the students' right to publish a newspaper as an exercise of free speech was not a primary concern. The publication was declared morally offensive and obscene. It was agreed that the production of *Hard Times* had been carried out in part on school property and with school equipment, and that the school authorities had a legal right to discipline the four students.

It could not be claimed that the students had broken any rules relating to student publications, since none existed in Granville. But Miller and Butler found justification for suspending the students in a New York State education law that permits suspension of "a pupil who is insubordinate, or disorderly, or whose conduct otherwise endangers the safety, morals, health or welfare of others."

So the punishment meted out to Donna, John, David, and Richard was a five-day suspension, to begin on February 1, a Thursday, and end the following Wednesday, February 7. The suspension could be reduced to three school days for any student who wrote an essay entitled "Potential Harm to People Caused by the Publication of Irresponsible and/or Obscene Writing." In addition, for the next month the four students were to spend their study periods in the administrative offices of the school, rather than in study halls with their fellow students. And Donna, the only senior involved, was to be deprived of senior privileges for the rest of the year.

Mager did not escape scot-free, either. He received a letter from Butler that said, in part, "Assuming that all you have reported is true, in my opinion your professional judgment was lacking the maturity and soundness I would have expected. . . ."

With punishment of the culprits decreed, the board of education mollified, and the offensive publication impounded, it appeared as if Granville High School's administration could settle back into its normal routine. But, in fact, its troubles were just beginning.

Richard Wolf conferred with the four students and their parents. Some of the parents, on first reading *Hard Times,* had been less than enthusiastic about it. John E. Jones, father of David, was said to have declared that he would break his son's neck if he became involved in another similar paper. Donna's mother had been quoted as saying the newspaper was "awful." But they had, in general, come to feel that the paper wasn't so terrible, after all—that it contained nothing that most high school students didn't already know and talk about. They felt much more strongly that their children were being unfairly punished, and they were entirely willing to help defend them.

On Tuesday, February 6, having spun the wheels of legal procedure with unusual speed, Wolf and Emery were in the United States District Court, Northern District of New York, in Albany. Despite the fact that the students' suspension period was almost over, they were applying to Judge James T. Foley for a temporary order restraining Butler, Miller, Tatko, and other members of the board of education—the defendants named in the application—from putting into effect the punishment decreed for the plaintiffs, Thomas, Tiedeman, Jones, and Williams.

The NYCLU also asked the court to declare that the plaintiffs had the right, under the First Amendment, to publish and sell their paper anywhere—a right that no New York law could deprive them of because of the Fourteenth Amendment. A further request of the court was for the expungement of any mention of suspension from the plaintiffs' school records.

Furthermore, the NYCLU wanted the court to prevent the defendants from interfering with any further production and sale of the newspaper, and to prevent punishment of students involved in it. And, finally, on behalf of the plaintiffs, the NYCLU wanted the return of the copies of *Hard Times* that Butler had taken from Mager's closet.

The three boys, still minors, were represented in the action by their parents. Donna, being of age, represented herself.

Judge Foley denied the plaintiffs' request for a temporary restraining order on the grounds that it was too late for such an order to have any effect. The plaintiffs, he pointed out, had already served four of their five days of suspension.

He did enjoin—stop—the writing of an essay on obscenity because, as he said, ". . . the Supreme Court is having great difficulty writing on that subject." And he suggested that the students' records be expunged of any mention of the suspensions and that Donna's senior privileges be restored. Only the second of his two suggestions was accepted.

The judge set February 21 as the date for the hearing. He also designated February 14 and 15 as dates for the taking of pretrial depositions, when both sides would question each other's potential witnesses under oath.

The pretrial examinations were preliminary skirmishes. The real battle was joined in Judge Foley's courtroom on February 21.

Richard Emery outlined the case for the plaintiffs. One argument was that while *Hard Times* might be considered offensive, it was not legally obscene and thus was protected by the First Amendment. Another was that since no rules existed concerning student publications at Granville High School, the students could not have broken any. Emery also claimed that *Hard Times* had caused no disturbance in the school and that nothing had really happened until Mrs. Tatko stirred things up. Still another argument was Emery's claim that the students' right of free expression was guaranteed both on and off school property, so it made no difference where the paper had been produced. He further contended that the school administrators' concern over the townspeople's reaction to *Hard Times* did not give them the right to punish the students.

A student's right of free speech, Emery argued, does not depend on whether the surrounding community likes or does not like what the student has said or written.

H. Wayne Judge, counsel for the defendants, had a number of arguments in his defensive arsenal. One was that, despite a warning, the students had produced a paper on school property, and that because of this the school officials had a legal right to suppress the paper and punish its producers. He also argued that while *Hard Times* might not be legally obscene for adults, it certainly was obscene for young readers, and if allowed to spread through the school would cause disorder and a breakdown of discipline. These factors alone, Counsel Judge claimed, justified punishment in accord with the New York State education law. A further defense claim was that *Hard Times* could be seen by the public as a school-connected publication, one injurious to the school's standing in the community.

The defendants' counsel also asked Judge Folcy to follow long-standing judicial tradition and refuse to involve his court in what was actually an educational problem best settled by trained school administrators.

Both sides, of course, depended on witnesses to bolster their arguments. The students, for example, testified firmly that they had not considered the meeting with Reed a warning not to publish. They had been careful, they said, to do all they could to disassociate *Hard Times* from the school, as Reed and Mager had suggested. Principal Butler, on the other hand, insisted that Reed had, through Tiedeman, warned the students not to publish a paper.

"Did Mr. Reed ever tell you that he had told the students not to publish the paper?" Emery asked Butler during cross-examination.

"No," Butler said.

"Did he ever tell you he wanted to review the paper or have some official review the paper before it was published—that he told [the students] that?"

Again Butler answered, "No."

Both sides spent a good deal of time on the question of obscenity. On this point, too, the principal was firm. "My opinion is that the paper is obscene as to minors."

In cross-examination Emery pressed Butler to define obscenity. And Butler, after a series of questions, said, "I do not believe I can give justice to a definition. . . . All I know is, I looked, I read, I consulted, I thought and concluded."

Later Emery questioned Butler about how he decided whether or not the publication had been produced on school premises. After much confusion, and intervention by the judge, Butler replied, "I will make a general statement that if it were produced outside the school I wouldn't get involved, wouldn't get concerned. When it starts infringing on school areas, I get concerned. . . ."

Emery then asked Butler how he expected the students to know they were "infringing on school areas," since Butler himself couldn't give a definite answer to what constituted school involvement.

"I don't know how they would know," Butler said.

Both sides also called on expert witnesses. The NYCLU submitted an affidavit from a professor of education at the State University of New York. His opinion was that there was no basis for any prediction that *Hard Times* would cause disruption or harm, and that no competent expert would venture such a prediction.

The defendants submitted affidavits from three experienced educators who had been asked to read *Hard Times*. One said the paper was obscene and that its publication could result in "fostering a breakdown of discipline" and be "disruptive of the educational process due to disputes that would be triggered among parent taxpayers." Another maintained that obscene materials serve no educational purpose; and that school authorities, representing the parents of all students, have the responsibility to regulate student publications. The third educator said that "permitting such publications in school could polarize the community with a concomitant disruption of the school program."

Finally, the taking of testimony, the reading of affidavits, and the face-to-face legal fencing was finished. Judge Foley asked each side to file a brief—a written summation of its arguments, buttressed by citations from judicial decisions in previous cases. From these briefs, and from the testimony given at the hearing, Judge Foley would make his decision.

In the brief he submitted, Emery relied heavily on the Supreme Court decision in the Tinker case. In that well-known case it had been ruled that freedom of student expression in school could be suppressed only if the administration could reasonably expect it to result in serious disruption of the school program. "Undifferentiated fear or apprehension of disturbance," the Court had said, "is not enough to overcome the right to freedom of expression." Emery, of course, had maintained throughout the hearing that there had been no disruption of the Granville school program, and that none could reasonably have been expected.

Judge Foley's decision was released on May 2. It, too, relied on the Tinker case. But in Judge Foley's opinion the Granville authorities *could* reasonably have expected that *Hard Times* would disrupt the school's program. He also accepted the defendants' claim that the students had been warned against publishing their paper. "The prohibition of *Hard Times*," he therefore declared, "and the punishment of the students for its publication . . . were reasonable restraints upon expression."

Judge Foley didn't waste much time on the argument that Granville had no right to punish the students in the absence of any rules regulating student publications. The Constitution, he wrote, does not require a specific rule for every "conceivable aspect of high school student conduct before school administrators can discipline." And he briskly avoided another issue by declaring that "this Court does not deem it necessary to become entangled in the illusive concept of obscenity."

Judge Foley made clear in his decision his reluctance to intervene in educational matters. The case he had just heard, he wrote, "in my judgment seems particularly one for solution within the public education system of New York, which is noted for its safeguards and reviews in matters of this kind." His decision was a vindication of the Granville school authorities' actions: The plaintiffs' pleas were "denied and dismissed."

Two months later Emery appealed this decision to the United States Court of Appeals for the Second District. The arguments he used were essentially the same he had presented to Judge Foley. His requests were the same.

The appeals court decision, written by Judge Irving R. Kaufman and published on October 15, 1979, also avoided the obscenity question. And it, too, did not rule on Emery's contention that the First Amendment protects student freedom of speech on school property. To the appeals court the crux of the matter was whether *Hard Times* had been produced inside the school or outside. The decision was definite and emphatic on that score.

Judge Kaufman had written that "all but an insignificant amount of relevant activity in this case was deliberately designed to take place beyond the schoolhouse gate.

Indeed, the appellants diligently labored to ensure that *Hard Times* was printed outside the school and that no copies were sold on school grounds. That a few articles were transcribed on school typewriters and the finished product secretly and unobtrusively stored in a teacher's closet do not alter the fact that *Hard Times* was conceived, executed, and distributed outside the school."

Having decided that point, the court went on to set some limits on official school authority. The decision states:

Public education in America enables our nation's youth to become responsible participants in a self-governing society. To perform this critical function effectively, professional educators must be accorded substantial discretion to oversee properly their myriad responsibilities. But our willingness to defer to the schoolmaster's expertise in administering school discipline rests, in large measure, upon the supposition that the arm of authority does not reach beyond the schoolhouse gate. . . . Where, as in the instant case, school officials bring their punitive power to bear on the publication and distribution of a newspaper off school grounds, that power must be cabined within the rigorous confines of the First Amendment, the ultimate safeguard of popular democracy. We hold that these limits have been exceeded in the case before us.

Responding to the NYCLU contention that school officials have no right to limit free expression because of community reaction, Judge Kaufman wrote:

We may not permit school administrators to seek approval of the community-at-large by punishing students for expressions that took place off school property. Nor may courts endorse such punishment because the populace would approve. The First Amendment will not abide the additional chill on protected expression that would inevitably emanate from such a practice.

The appeals court, finding another danger that could "emanate from such a practice," declared that since school administrators have a built-in interest in maintaining tranquility in and around their institutions, they tend to run their institutions in a way their communities are likely to approve. And this, the appeals court said, could lead school authorities to act according to local prejudices rather than to educational and legal standards.

Commenting on what the Granville school officials' actions could lead to, Judge Kaufman wrote:

It is not difficult to imagine the lengths to which school authorities could take the power they have exercised in the case before us. If they possessed this power, it would be within their discretion to suspend a student who purchases an issue of *National Lampoon,* the inspiration for *Hard Times,* at a neighborhood newsstand and lends it to a school friend. And, it is conceivable that school officials could consign a student to a segregated study hall because he and a classmate watched an X-rated film on his living room cable television. While these activities are certainly the proper subjects of parental discipline, the First Amendment forbids public school administrators and teachers from regulating the material to which a child is exposed after he leaves school each afternoon. Parents still have a role to play in bringing up their children. . . .

The three-word conclusion of the decision was "reversed and remanded." It meant that the school authorities' actions had been declared unconstitutional. It would be up to Judge Foley to decide what relief the students were entitled to.

Before he could act, the Granville school officials decided to appeal the decision, not only in the hope of vindicating their own actions but also to establish a precedent. They filed a petition asking the Supreme Court to judge the case.

In January 1980, the Supreme Court refused, automatically letting stand the appeals court decision.

On May 19, 1980, Judge Foley ordered Granville High School authorities to stop interfering with the off-campus publication of *Hard Times.* He also ordered them to return to the four students the copies Butler had taken from Mager's closet.

The NYCLU had not succeeded in its attempt to gain for students the unqualified right of free speech within the confines of a school. But a lawyer who had defended many publishers and writers in First Amendment cases called the Granville decision a "sweeping affirmation of the rights of high school students in their non-scholastic lives."

Of the case, Emery said, "This should mean, for example, that high school underground papers published off campus are now safe. Except to the extent that kids are regulated by their parents, they now have the same rights to express themselves outside of school as adults do."

10

The Wishkah Valley Girls

Three high school girls in the little dairy farming community of Wishkah Valley, in the state of Washington, were the subjects of a feature story in the *Star-News* of the nation's capital on Wednesday, September 9, 1973. The story was illustrated by a picture of fourteen-year-old Delores Darrin, wearing a padded football jersey and helmet, under the headline "YES, DELORES IS A GUARD."

In large type beside the picture was a quotation from Delores's sixteen-year-old sister, Carol. "None of the other guys at school would turn out, so we figured the team needed us," Carol had said. The third girl mentioned in the story was the Darrin sisters' friend, Kathy Tosland.

All three of them were expected to make sports history when they played on their school's varsity football team in its first game of the season the following Saturday. The controversy that would keep them off the field that day made history of another kind—legal history.

There were only 102 students in Wishkah Valley High School that year. Forty-five of them were boys, but of that number only ten had appeared to try for a place on the Loggers, the school's football team. Another ten boys, who had already won their football letters and were eligible to play, apparently regarded the Loggers as unworthy of their time or the rigors of training. Their attitude disturbed John Clark, the school's young football coach, but he understood the reason for it. So did his assistant, Dennis Darrin, brother of Delores and Carol. The Loggers had been on a long losing streak that had demoralized the whole school. For eighteen games in a row they had gone down to defeat with scores like 42 to 6 and 48 to 0.

Clark had hoped the new season would be a better one. He was ready to do anything within his power to make it so. But he couldn't think of anything to do except keep his boys at work on their preseason drills—and hope the sight of their faithful practice sessions would inspire at least some of the other eligible players to join them.

By August 29, after three weeks of drill, Clark still had only his original ten boys to work with. At least one of them would almost certainly fail to meet varsity standards. And though it was true that the local league in which Wishkah Valley competed was made up of eight-player squads, most of the league's schools could suit up as many as thirty or forty boys on an afternoon.

The first game of the season was just two weeks away.

The Loggers' future seemed hopeless.

Carol Darrin, a senior, and Kathy Tosland, a junior, had been concerned about the team for some time. Carol's brother had been talking about it at the supper table, worrying because so few boys had turned out. Kathy's two brothers were equally worried—they were both on the team.

"I'd like to try out for it myself," Carol said suddenly on that late August day.

"Why don't we?" Kathy said.

The next instant they were heading together for the coach's office.

Coach Clark didn't laugh at the surprising suggestion the girls made to him. He knew both of them, knew they'd worked since they were small on their fathers' farms. Dennis Darrin had once said his sisters could toss bales of hay around as well as any hand his father had ever had. Clark also knew that Kathy liked most sports and that Carol liked track and had played basketball for two years.

Kathy wasn't very big, of course—not more than 130 pounds. But three of Clark's football players were smaller than she was. Carol, considerably larger, was about five and a half feet tall and weighed 170 pounds.

"Delores has been sick," Carol said of her sophomore sister, "but we could get her to come out with us, too, in a couple of days."

Clark knew Delores stood a strapping 5 foot 9 inches and weighed over 200 pounds. "All right," the coach said, reaching for jerseys and shoulder pads. "We'll see what you can do."

The jerseys he handed them were black. The boys wore white ones. But the black jerseys were the only ones he had that weren't full of holes, and they were a good excuse to put the girls in uniforms of a distinctive color. Now if someone in a black jersey got knocked down, he'd know it was one of the girls even if he couldn't see her face.

The team members were dumbfounded when they realized that the two figures crossing the field with the coach weren't boys. Of course they recognized Carol and Kathy when they came close enough. Everybody in the Wishkah Valley school knew everybody else. They'd all grown up together. But the boys couldn't imagine what the girls were doing on the field, and in football jerseys.

Clark told them, and they had to believe him. The coach was always serious.

The boys didn't like it. "It was sort of hard on them at first," Carol said long afterward, remembering that day. "They felt hurt, I guess—having girls think they could help their team."

But the only reaction the boys let themselves show was righteous indignation. After practice—the girls couldn't do a push-up at all, but Clark said they could come back the next day, anyway—the boys elected a committee and sent it to the coach with their protests. They had several:

They wouldn't be able to hit a girl, and it wasn't possible to play tackle football without hitting other players.

Other teams wouldn't want to play against a team that had girls on it.

A boy wouldn't be able to report that he'd been struck in the genitals, and needed attention, since he couldn't mention such a thing with girls nearby.

The boys would have to watch their language in front of girls, and they wouldn't be able to play their best if they couldn't cuss and swear when they felt like it.

Coach Clark listened to the members of the committee. Then he said, "I'd hoped more of the boys would turn out. But if they're too busy drinking, or whatever, we'll see if the girls can do a man's work."

He made that same answer to everyone who, by the next

morning, was hurling arguments at him in the teachers' lounge and in the outside community.

"Girls should be at home after school, where they belong—not out on the football field!" he was frequently told.

The mother of one of the boys on the team, backing up the boys' insistence that they wouldn't be able to hit a girl, said firmly, "My son wouldn't be allowed to!"

The one argument Clark paid serious attention to was the one rising out of concern for the girls' safety. "It's dangerous for them to be out there," many people said. "They could get hurt!"

Clark shared their concern, especially about the possibility of an injurious blow to the breast. So he contrived a breast protection for each girl, using a pair of knee pads, foam rubber, tape, and ingenuity.

Then he settled down to the girls' training. By the third day there were three of them, as Carol had told him there would be. Delores was shy and hadn't much wanted to come out on the field with the others, but they had convinced her that it was her duty to the school to try out for the team.

The girls all tended to overestimate their strength at first and became discouraged when their farm-trained muscles couldn't adapt to new demands. Sometimes, when their muscles ached badly, they cried. Sometimes they complained that the boys hit them too hard—and did it on purpose.

But they didn't give up. It took them a week, but they finally managed the push-up. Gradually their muscles hardened and their stamina increased. Soon they were complaining that the boys weren't hitting them hard enough. They wanted to be hit as hard as the boys hit one another.

The girls were beginning to hit back, too. And when the boys forgot their presence and swore, they didn't even notice. Practice sessions were returning to normal, to the pattern they had followed before the girls arrived.

One day Delores rammed into the practice dummy being held by the school's 210-pound custodian. "She hit me so hard she hurt my arm!" he said admiringly. From that moment on it seemed likely that Delores, at least, could be a valuable player against even a husky opponent.

Some of the older boys then began showing the girls their own favorite tricks for success on the field. They were coaching them, as they might have coached freshmen boys. They tried to correct the girls' mistakes, and the girls listened and tried to follow their advice. The thirteen Wishkah Valley players were becoming a team.

If the girls were really going to be on the team, how-ever, Clark had to take care of a few details first. He talked to the girls' parents to make sure they approved. None of them was upset at the idea of a girl playing football with boys.

"We're really excited about the whole thing," the Darrin girls' father said.

And Mrs. Darrin said, "I think it's neat! I wish I'd done the same thing when I was in school."

Then Clark went through the routines necessary before he could fill out affidavits for the WIAA. This organization, the Washington Interscholastic Activities Association, regulated all interscholastic sports in the state. It required every participating student to attend a specific number of practice sessions, pass a medical examination, and fill out an insurance policy. So Clark made sure that Delores and Carol and Kathy, as well as nine of his boy players—one had failed to measure up to varsity standards—met all those requirements.

As the first game of the season approached, hopes soared. For the first time in many long months there was talk about a possible victory for Wishkah Valley High.

The reporter who interviewed the team members for the story that appeared in the Washington, D.C., newspaper on the Wednesday before the game asked one boy, "How did you feel when the girls first began to show you what they could do?"

By then the boy could answer that question honestly. "It kind of hurt our pride at first," he said. "But it took a lot of guts for them to turn out. And," he added, "we've got to have them."

On the Thursday before the game, Coach Clark received a message from the school board. The board had just been informed, the message said, that WIAA regulations prohibited women from taking part in a competitive football event involving men.

The members of the board were sorry, they told Clark. They were in favor of the girls playing. But the WIAA had warned them that if its ruling was ignored, Wishkah Valley would forfeit all football games and be prevented from taking part in any other interscholastic sports events. The board members were therefore ordering Coach Clark to leave the girls out of the lineup.

Coach Clark had to obey. On Saturday the three girls sat on the sidelines throughout the long grim afternoon. Their teammates were no match for the opposition. The score for Wishkah Valley's nineteenth consecutive loss was 78 to 8.

In the small city of Aberdeen, not far away, attorney John Wolfe and other members of the ACLU of Washington had been following the recent events at Wishkah Valley with interest. The state had recently become one of the thirty states to ratify the proposed Equal Rights Amendment, which had been passed overwhelmingly by Congress the year before. At the same time, the Washington state legislature had put the full force of its own authority behind the ERA's protection of women's rights by adding to its state constitution an article declaring: "Equality of rights and responsibilities under the law shall not be denied or abridged on account of sex."

The Women's Rights Committee of the ACLU of Washington shortly thereafter had distributed a statement expressing the organization's opinion of how the new article applied to sports. It said the organization "considers unequal provision of athletic resources on the basis of sex to be constitutionally impermissible."

The ACLU members also had been keeping track of the various new court decrees granting women the right to play with men, or compete against them, in such sports as golfing, skiing, and tennis. They knew no decree had yet been handed down as to women's rights in the contact team sport of football, and they hoped the courts soon would have to face that issue. A case involving football played in public high schools, they believed, could be especially significant, since high school football was funded by public money. For that reason, they now looked to the Wishkah Valley school board to bring an action against the WIAA to show, as one member put it, "that some school authorities do not share the sexist notions of the WIAA, and are acting to combat such sexism."

But the school board felt unable to make a move against the organization that could destroy the school's whole interscholastic program. John Wolfe therefore went to Wishkah Valley and talked to the girls and their parents, and to John Clark and the school authorities. He offered, as a cooperating attorney of the ACLU, to take the girls' case to a state court. Its costs, he added, would be met by the ACLU Foundation.

Kathy's parents said they didn't want her to be involved in a lawsuit, but the Darrins enthusiastically accepted Wolfe's offer. And the members of the school board, who understood they would be named defendants along with the WIAA, were equally enthusiastic. They said they would testify in court that they were in favor of the girls playing and would have permitted them to do so if not for the WIAA's threat.

On the eve of Wishkah Valley's second game of the season, Wolfe appeared in Gray County Superior Court, in the tiny town of Montesano. The plaintiffs he represented were "Mr. and Mrs. Russell Darrin, on behalf of Delores Darrin and Carol Darrin and all others similarly situated." He was thus bringing a class action that included all girls who, like Carol and Delores, had proved themselves qualified to play high school varsity football.

But first he hoped to get the three girls on the field for the following day's game. So he asked Judge John W. Schumaker for a restraining order on the WIAA—an order that would prevent it from restricting the girls' play until their case was settled. Judge Schumaker said no emergency existed to warrant such an order and promptly denied it. Then he set down the case for a full hearing at a date some two weeks away.

That week Wishkah Valley lost its twentieth straight game 36 to 14. On the following Monday the girls turned out again for practice, as they had done daily all the week before. No one could prevent them from doing that. And they meant to be in as good shape as possible on the day they were finally allowed to play—a day they felt sure would come.

At the start of the two-day hearing, both sides were ready with their arguments and their witnesses. One of the chief arguments presented by the WIAA's counsel was that a "unisex approach" to sports could jeopardize the women's athletic programs WIAA encouraged. Those programs involved more than a dozen interscholastic sports, including basketball, field hockey, soccer, and flag football, a non-contact game described as "similar in nature to football."

And it was pointed out that although a school could "provide an interscholastic program for girls which could be offered under WIAA rules," Wishkah Valley had not done so.

What the WIAA stood for, as its counsel explained, was "separate but equal" opportunities for both boy and girl athletes, and its officials believed this was for the girls' benefit. Their argument hinged on the generally accepted fact that boys were in most cases stronger and more muscular than girls, and it went like this: If girls were allowed to join boys' teams, boys would of course have to be allowed to join girls' teams. Boys would then replace girls on all the "best" and most competitive teams, especially in such strength-demanding sports as football. Thus girls would be cheated out of the exercise, the pleasure of competition, and the prestige that interscholastic sports could give them.

Among the WIAA's witnesses were educational authorities who made statements they seemed to regard as beyond contradiction. One such statement was "There are some activities indigenous to girls and some activities indigenous to boys."

The director of health for Seattle's schools said she felt girls and boys should not compete in tackle football, and in answer to Wolfe's "Why?" she replied, "I think it's inappropriate."

Another argument in WIAA's defense was one Clark had often heard: A male athlete's sense of chivalry would inhibit him when he was faced by female opponents.

"I just wouldn't want to hit a girl at all," a 210-pound Elma High School senior testified.

"I've been taught not to hit girls," a second male athlete declared. "It just wouldn't feel right."

Neither of those boys, Coach Clark pointed out afterward, had ever played against girls. "So they could only speculate," he said, "as to their reactions."

Clark, of course, was one of Wolfe's witnesses. Like others Wolfe called to the stand, he testified that his three girl players were able to give as good as they got in an aggressive game. He emphasized that the girls had met all the WIAA's requirements and—if only they were boys— would certainly be recognized as full-fledged members of the Wishkah Valley team.

The Darrin sisters testified, too. Delores, still shy, wasn't very comfortable on the stand. Carol was less bothered by the questions of the WIAA's lawyers even when, as she said later, "they tried to give me a hard time. But I've grown up in a tough family, having to hold my own against two brothers and four sisters, so they didn't scare me."

Wolfe, in his brief, then outlined the history of sex discrimination in the United States as one of "legal disabilities, judicial nonchalance, social and cultural stereotypes and paternalistic attitudes." Before the Civil War, he pointed out, women's legal status had been like that of blacks under the slave codes. "Men controlled the behavior of both their slaves and their wives," he said. And he quoted Tennyson's famous nineteenth-century description of a wife's place in the eyes of her husband: "Something better than his dog, a little dearer than his horse."

But when woman was put on a pedestal, Wolfe went on, her freedom wasn't necessarily increased. The pedestal, as one jurist had recently pointed out, "has all too often, upon closer inspection, been revealed as a cage." Laws passed to "protect" a woman for her role as wife and mother, Wolfe added, also often served to limit her freedom as a person.

After listing recent laws that did protect women's rights in the worlds of education, politics, economics, and even the traditionally masculine world of sports, Wolfe said it was still possible for the courts to deny them their rights as athletes. One such denial had been handed down not long before by an Oregon judge who upheld a sports commission ruling that refused a woman the wrestling license she sought. The judge said the commission had acted on the authority of a "predominantly masculine legislature," whose members had watched women invade "practically every activity formerly considered suitable and appropriate for men only." The judge had therefore defended the commission's intention to keep for men "at least one island on the sea of life . . . that would be impregnable to the assault of women."

But the Supreme Court of the United States had handed down a decision only a few months ago, Wolfe went on, declaring that all classifications by sex, "like classifications based upon race, alienage and national origin, are inherently suspect." By a "suspect" classification, Wolfe explained, the Supreme Court had meant one into which an individual was locked by the accident of birth, and that bore no relation to the individual's ability to perform or contribute to society. Suspect classification, the Supreme Court had emphasized, could result in a whole class of people being regarded as inferior. And the Court had decreed that no state or federal law based on a suspect classification could be upheld unless a "compelling state interest" was at stake.

No "compelling state interest" would be served, Wolfe then claimed, by preventing girls from playing football just because they were girls. "The time has come," he said, "when the judiciary must enter the mainstream of contemporary political and social opinion, and respond to the critical nature of sexism." Refusing to do so out of "solicitous concern for the well-being of women," he concluded, could not excuse depriving women of their "full legal rights as human beings."

Judge Schumaker didn't announce his decision when

the hearing ended. Before it closed, however, he asked some questions about the class action Wolfe was bringing. The questions suggested that the judge might be planning to settle the case in favor of the Darrin girls, but without including "all others similarly situated." He sometimes gave the impression that he thought Wolfe was trying to thrust weak, fragile, untrained girls out onto a football field, although Wolfe felt he had clearly described the class he meant as including only those girls who could qualify for a varsity football team.

"If a girl can't quality for the team," Coach Clark had said, "then she won't make it and, therefore, won't play."

But the decision Judge Schumaker rendered, about a week later, didn't distinguish between the Darrin girls and any "class." It simply upheld the WIAA's regulation against girls playing varsity football with boys.

The judge's reasoning followed that of the WIAA: High school girls should and could have their own athletic programs. And permitting girls to "play contact football, involving the corresponding right of boys to join all girls' teams," would make development of those programs "extremely difficult, if not impossible."

Wolfe immediately decided, with the agreement of the Darrins, to appeal the judge's decision to the state supreme court.

While his appeal was under way—appeals tend to take a long time—Carol and Delores turned down offers to join professional women's wrestling teams. They continued to practice on the football field for as long as the season lasted. The season ended as badly as it had begun.

In the spring Coach Clark wrote an article for the Seattle *Post-Intelligencer* in which he described what had happened in Wishkah Valley the previous fall. "Perhaps by next year," his article ended, "we will have the legalities taken care of. Then watch out, teams, here we come."

Carol was graduated at the end of that school year. Delores continued to practice faithfully with the team during the following season, although, with the appeal still undecided, she was not allowed to play against other schools. By her senior year, however, she decided that there were more rewarding things to do with her afternoons, and she dropped football.

Two things important to this story happened during the fall of Delores's senior year. One was noticed chiefly in Wishkah Valley: More boys turned out for the football team, backed by a school spirit that seemed to have been recharged, and Wishkah Valley won some games. Many people thought the girls had brought about the change.

The other event had a far wider influence. On September 25, 1975, the Supreme Court of the State of Washington, sitting *en banc*—that is, with all its nine judges taking part—handed down its decision on the hearing that had finally taken place before it. In two concurring opinions, the judges reversed the lower court decision of Judge Schumaker.

The majority opinion, signed by five of the judges, simply held that denying high school students the right to play on a school's football team, "solely on the ground" that they were girls, was "discrimination based on sex" and therefore prohibited.

The second opinion had been signed by the other four judges "with some qualms," as they wrote, and only because they believed no other decision was possible under the state's Equal Rights Amendment. They doubted whether the people who had enacted that law "fully contemplated and appreciated" the results it might have in such a case as this. "Nevertheless," they wrote, "in sweeping language they embedded the principle of the ERA in our constitution, and it is beyond the authority of this court to modify the people's will. So be it."

Thousands of girls and women all over the country rejoiced at the decision. Other females—as well as males—were less happy about it. Many coaches and school officials soberly predicted that it could mean the eventual demise of all school athletics. Others, not quite so disturbed, were nevertheless concerned because they realized the Darrin case had not settled the whole question of women's place in sports.

"It is unclear how the court would have decided this case had Wishkah Valley provided opportunity for women to compete on all-female teams," a statement from the national ACLU office pointed out. " 'Separate but equal' cases are yet to be litigated."

Even the ACLU of Washington State, responsible for what so many were heralding as an important civil rights victory, was still struggling with that separate-but-equal problem. The following spring, after lengthy discussions, it finally issued a statement of its policy on women and athletics.

The organization supported a woman's right to play on a men's team when no women's program in the sport existed, or when a women's program didn't offer her enough opportunity for challenging competition. It also recognized the "ultimate goal to be the fullest coeducational participation in athletics." But it declared that "quality women's programs currently may provide the most equitable opportunity for women in athletics" and held that such programs should be "established by all groups and organizations which use public funds."

If an existing women's team doesn't provide the kind of tough competition one of its members is capable of, should that one woman be allowed to play on a men's team instead? Can men's and women's programs that are described as separate but equal ever be truly equal? Those questions can still arouse argument today.

In the meantime, statistics show a steady increase in the number of girls involved in sports. By 1980 girls made up 33 percent of all high school athletes—six times the number they had been in the early 1970s.

Women's physical strength seemed to be increasing, too, and many attributed that to more and better sports training during the adolescent years. Although the first group of female cadets at West Point, in 1976, could do an average of less than one pull-up each, the 1979 entrants were able to chin the bar an average of two and one-half times.

Carol Darrin, whose only sports interest by 1981 was off-the-road racing, has her own standard for measuring the success of what she started the day she told Kathy she'd like to try out for the football team: In the school near her home there are many more sports for girls, and many more girls in sports, than there were when she was a Wishkah Valley senior. She thinks that's a good thing.

And she is glad she didn't just *wish* she could try out for the team. Instead she and Delores and Kathy had actually done so. "Don't ever be scared to do what you want to do" is what she tells any girl who asks her advice today.

11

Student v. Kentucky

When twenty-year-old Steve Ashton drove into Hazard, Kentucky, on a March day in 1963, he parked in front of the union hall headquarters of the region's striking coal miners. Earlier that year, he had been in Hazard briefly, delivering the first donations of food and clothing he and other Oberlin College students had collected for the strikers and their families. Between that visit and this one, Oberlin students had sent the strikers a truckload of donations, and now Steve's Volkswagen carried still more gifts from the Ohio college campus. This time Steve planned to stay in Hazard long enough to learn all he could about what he called "the most important labor protest in recent years."

There were already several out-of-town young people at the union hall. Most of them were other college students who had also come to Hazard out of sympathy with what was happening there. Most of them, like Steve, had seen a December 1962 CBS documentary that showed the gaunt, determined faces of the strikers and those of their wives and hungry children. The documentary had informed Americans that money, food, and clothing for the strikers' families could be sent to the office of the local newspaper, the Hazard *Herald,* to be distributed from there by a citizens committee. But Steve had learned that not all of the donations received had been given to the families of strikers, and he was therefore delivering the Oberlin contributions directly to the union hall.

He slept on the floor of the hall that night. The next day he talked to some of the strike leaders and told them he wanted to make a close-range study of the strike and send it to strike sympathizers all over the country, along with a plea for continued help.

Steve knew he had convinced the men that he could be useful to them when they took him along to the home of Herb Stacey, a retired miner, and asked Stacey to put him up. "And that's all there was to it," Steve said later. "The Staceys simply took me in. I'll never forget them." For Steve Ashton that was the beginning of what he would always recall as "an enriching, rewarding experience"— although it landed him in jail and involved him in a long legal battle that did not end until it reached the Supreme Court of the United States.

The idealistic enthusiasm Steve brought to that experience was one he shared with many young people of the sixties, a decade of marked political and social ferment. On campuses all over the country, students were deeply concerned about the causes they believed in—school and restaurant desegregation, for example, and voting rights for southern blacks. They organized marches. They held mass meetings and sit-ins. They protested against Congress's HUAC, the House Un-American Activities Committee, for what they regarded as its "smear tactics" investigations.

Steve, a junior philosophy major, had helped organize such programs at Oberlin. Also, he had taken part in the student exchange between Oberlin and what had long been an all-black college in Mississippi. Like other young political activists, he had often been labeled Communist by conservative-minded Americans. He knew the label was common in Hazard, where the *Herald* used it frequently for "outsiders" like himself.

Herb Stacey's home provided Steve with just the sort of information he was looking for. Stacey's living room opened onto what had been a popular beer tavern. Now, when few men could afford the price of a drink, Stacey's tavern was chiefly a meeting place for strikers who matter-of-factly stacked their guns at the door when they came in. They had armed themselves, they told Steve, after four of them had been shot at from a speeding car as they walked a picket line the month before.

Steve often went out with the men, who liked to call themselves the Roving Pickets of Eastern Kentucky. On cold, rainy nights he joined them when they manned picket lines at the entrance to mines being operated by "scabs"—nonunion members or union members who had refused to join the strike. With them he drove up into the hills to deliver supplies to isolated strikers' families. On the way back to Hazard from one of those trips, they stopped at a mountain cabin for a pint of colorless liquid, and Steve was given his first jolting swallow of "Kentucky white lightning." On Sunday mornings he listened to the fiery sermons preached by a minister who was one of the strike's most stalwart leaders.

Everywhere he went, he made notes on what he saw and heard. Everywhere he went, he took photographs with the camera he had borrowed from his college roommate.

Steve thought of the report he was writing as "a letter to my friends." He called it "Notes on a Mountain Strike." Its heroes were the striking miners, whom he described as "fighting for the freedom from hunger." Its villains were the coal mine owners and their supporters. It was this report that would lead to his arrest.

Until the 1930s, Steve wrote, the region's mine owners had grown rich while miners worked a twelve-hour day in dangerous underground conditions for a wage of $2. Then the UMW—more properly the UMWA, the United Mine Workers of America—had sent organizers into eastern Kentucky, and after a long struggle most of the mine owners had signed union contracts. The contracts guaranteed miners a daily wage of over $20, safer working conditions, and payments to their union's welfare fund of 40 cents for each ton of coal mined. Those 40-cent-a-ton payments provided the miners with their first health-care programs and supported their new hospitals.

The area had never become really prosperous, Steve wrote, but for a time the union contracts meant that "a miner could live well and send his kids through school."

Then the mine owners had learned how to rid themselves of the contracts they had so stubbornly resisted: They retained control of their costly sorting and shipping equipment, but they started leasing portions of their land to "truck mine" operators, men whose only equipment was a truck or two. Those nonunionized operators then hired unemployed men, for wages as little as $3 or $4 a day, to dig coal out of the plots they had leased. They sold the coal to the property owner for $3 a ton, and the owner sorted the coal and shipped it to customers who paid him twice that price or more. As soon as a big mine owner could supply all his customers with coal bought from his truck operators, he closed down his own mine and thus terminated his union contract. That left dozens of union members jobless and cut off support to the union's welfare fund.

"This strike started in September 1962 and is now 7 months old," Steve wrote. ". . . the UMW is not helping organize the truck mines and not aiding the strikers in any way." He had not been able to learn, he added, whether the UMW could not afford strike support or whether, as some said, it had "deserted the area."

"The pickets get fed only by contributions sent from outside," he pointed out, ". . . and it is our responsibility to help them, for if the operators here are permitted to keep a man down and hungry, then companies will keep men down and hungry elsewhere."

His "Notes" named several persons he believed bore a particularly heavy responsibility for the miners' plight. Among them were Charles E. Combs, a miner owner who was also sheriff of Perry County, of which Hazard was the county seat; Hazard's police chief, Sam L. "Bud" Luttrell; and Mrs. W. P. Nolan, editor of the Hazard *Herald,* which she and her husband owned. The specific statements Steve made about those three persons were the basis of the charges against him.

Of Sheriff Combs as a mine owner, Steve wrote that he "has publicly bragged of making $60,000 in sixty days." Later in his "Notes" he added,

The High Sheriff has hired 72 deputies at one time, more than ever before in history; most of them hired because they wanted to carry guns. . . . In a recent court decision he was fined $5,000 for intentionally blinding a boy with tear-gas and beating him while he was locked in a jail cell with his hands cuffed. The boy lost the sight of one eye completely and is nearly blind in the other. Before the trial Sheriff Combs offered the boy $75,000 to keep it out of court, but he refused. Then for a few thousand dollars Combs probably bought off the jury. . . . Combs is now indicted for the murder of a man—voluntary manslaughter. Yet he is still the law in this county and has the support of the rich man because he will fight the pickets and the strike.

Steve's comments about Mrs. Nolan, the editor of the *Herald,* had to do with the donations sent to her office for the strikers. Steve wrote:

Mrs. W. P. Nolan is vehemently against labor—she has said she would rather give the incoming aid to the merchants in town than to the miners. Apparently that is what she has done, for only $1,100 of the money has come to the pickets, and none of the food and clothes. They are now either still under lock and key, or have been given out to the scabs and others.

What he wrote about Sheriff Combs and Mrs. Nolan had been told to him by the strikers, in whose honesty he had complete trust. They also told him that Police Chief Luttrell "has a job on the side" of guarding a mine owner's home for $100 a week. "It's against the law for a peace officer to take private jobs," Steve added.

But Steve wrote something about Luttrell's police force that he claimed to know from personal experience:

I witnessed a plot to kill the one pro-strike city policeman on the Hazard force. Three of the other cops were after him while he was on night duty. It took 5 pickets guarding him all night long to keep him from getting killed, but they could not prevent him from being fired, which he was three weeks ago.

Steve's "Notes," when they were finally finished and typed, filled seven single-spaced pages. Another page carried his request to his readers. "If you decide to do anything which may be of help, please let me know," it said, and gave the address—Tougaloo College, Tougaloo, Mississippi—where he planned to spend the rest of the semester. Tougaloo was the all-black college where he had been an exchange student and where he now hoped to study again with a professor who was a leader in the decade's civil-rights movement.

By March 26, a Tuesday, Steve had mimeographed 300 copies of each of his typed pages. That evening, at a table in Herb Stacey's tavern, he began assembling those copies into what was usually called, in court testimony, his "pamphlet." Shortly before midnight, two police patrolmen came in. Steve knew them only by sight, but it wasn't unusual for the police to pay a visit to Stacey's. One of them asked him what the papers on the table were.

"Reading material," Steve told him. "Do you want to see one?"

And when the man said yes, Steve showed a copy of his "Notes" to each of the officers. Some minutes later, after they had glanced at them, he asked for their return, but the men left with the pamphlets in their pockets.

Early the next morning, in the Stacey living room, Steve was still collating and addressing his "Notes" when a third patrolman arrived and asked for a copy. Steve gave him one, too, and the officer departed immediately.

Then, about an hour later, Chief Luttrell and two of his men entered the tavern. The two men remained there. The chief walked through the open door into the living room and stopped in front of Steve.

"Are you Steve Ashton?" he asked.

"Yes," Steve answered.

The brief conversation that followed was reported by

Chief Luttrell in his court testimony. According to that testimony, it went like this:

"Then I have a warrant for your arrest on the charge of criminal libel."

"What are you talking about?"

"This stuff you've got right here in front of you."

"Why, this doesn't hurt anybody!"

"The heck it don't!"

The chief then piled all of Steve's "Notes" into the cardboard box Steve had been using and announced that he was seizing it as evidence. He and his officers marched Steve outside and shoved him into one of the several police cars waiting there. Minutes later Steve was standing before a judge at police headquarters.

A formal hearing on the charges against him would be held the following morning, the judge told Steve, and unless he could post a bond he would remain in jail until then. The judge added that Steve was entitled to one phone call.

Posting a bond was out of the question. Steve telephoned his father in New York.

It wasn't an easy conversation. Court Ashton found it hard to believe that Steve was calling from a police station. But when the circumstances were clear to him, he said he would leave for Hazard as soon as possible and would probably arrive there the next day.

Then a still-incredulous Steve was conducted to the second-floor room that served as Hazard's jail. There were bunks for some twenty men in the big, bare room, but it had less than a dozen inmates that morning. Who was he? they all wanted to know. Had he been booked for vagrancy, too? Or picked up drunk? And did he have any cigarettes?

The first of the day's parade of visiting strikers soon arrived. They told Steve not to worry—that they were already making plans to raise his bond. Then one of them pointed out that the top of the hill sloping up behind the building was visible through the window high in one wall of the room.

"A gun aimed down from up there could kill you if you was in line with it, opposite that window," he said. "So you be sure to sleep on a bunk right *under* the window. That way no bullet could get at you. Remember that now!"

"I'll remember," Steve said, not sure whether to laugh at the melodramatic advice or take it seriously. But that night he did sleep directly beneath the window.

By the hour set for his hearing the next morning, Steve's father still hadn't arrived. The judge postponed the hearing until the following day, Friday.

In Thursday's *Herald* the story of Steve's arrest appeared under a headline stretching across two pages: "COLLEGE YOUTH WRITING OF COALFIELDS LABOR WOES HELD HERE FOR LIBEL." It described Steve as "a handsome cleancut looking young man with thick, wavy black hair. Of average build, he wears heavy horn-rimmed spectacles." It said he had come from Oberlin and Tougaloo colleges—it pointed out that Tougaloo was a "member of the United Negro College Fund"—and that he was "one of the great influx of college students and would-be writers who have come to this section."

He had written a "letter," it said, which "would be mailed to persons all over the nation adding more false impressions to the already distorted 'image' that the general public in other states has regarding East Kentucky mountain people.

"Much of Ashton's information," the *Herald* declared, "was of the nature that it could have been gleaned from the pages of Progressive Labor . . . the communist sheet."

The story didn't quote what it called "the alleged libelous statements" the letter made about the *Herald*'s editor, the police chief, and the county sheriff, but it did say those people were responsible for the charges brought against Steve Ashton. And it quoted the judge as saying the maximum fine for criminal libel was $5,000 and the maximum sentence twelve months in jail.

"Depending on the results of Friday's hearing, Ashton could be bound over to the May term of the Grand Jury for possible indictment and trial in Circuit Court," the *Herald* told its readers. "Since Ashton's arrest," it concluded, "numerous pickets have flooded to the jail to visit."

The next morning, Steve's hearing took place. His father had arrived and was present. So was a local lawyer hastily brought in to represent Steve.

It was all over very quickly. The judge said the charges against Steve would be heard by the grand jury, which was not scheduled to meet until late in May. Then he released Steve on a $2,000 bail bond the strikers had raised by taking out property bonds on their homes and on land that had been in one man's family for generations.

Steve was free to leave. And he had submitted to his father's demand to return to New York, rather than go to Tougaloo College as he had planned.

On his way south, Court Ashton had flown to Louisville, because its commercial airport was the one closest to Hazard. There he had hired the pilot and the small plane that had brought him to the little Perry County airstrip. The same plane was scheduled to take the Ashtons back to Louisville.

Several strikers' cars were waiting for them when they emerged from police headquarters. So were cars from the offices of the sheriff and the police chief, and several vehicles crowded with men the strikers called "goons"— armed supporters of the mine owners.

Two strikers, a father and son Steve had come to know, took Steve and his father in their car and started off for the airstrip. All the other cars started at the same time, some of them ahead of the Ashtons' car, some behind. Sirens sounded. Horns honked. There were taunting shouts from the cars of the mine owners' men and answering shouts from the strikers. The "hootin' and hollerin' " reminded Steve, he said later, of the bloody Kentucky-mountain feuds that kept hatreds alive for generations.

Some of the goons' cars quickly passed all the others and raced ahead. They were at the airstrip when the Ashtons' car came within sight of it, their guns firing in the direction of the waiting plane.

As Steve and his father watched, the plane's pilot revved up his motor and roared off into the sky. The driver of the Ashtons' car didn't wait to see the plane disappear. Swinging his car around in a tight circle, he drove away at top speed.

The cars of the sheriff's forces and those of the police tore after him. But the Ashtons' car was still ahead of its pursuers when it reached the Perry County line and crossed into adjoining Pike County.

"We'll be all right now," the Ashtons' driver said, slowing down. "They all know better than to try anything outside their own county." Then he drove the Ashtons to Pikeville, the county seat, where they were able to obtain transportation to the big Louisville airport.

Steve had had very little time to think during the past few days. He had plenty of time during the flight to New York, and a good deal to think about.

He faced a possible year in jail for criminal libel, a charge that was strange to him. He'd heard often enough of ordinary libel, a charge tried in a civil court and for which a convicted person would have to pay damages. But criminal libel? A form of libel regarded as a crime, to be tried in a criminal court and for which a convicted person could be sent to prison? Steve supposed the Kentucky legal system must permit such a charge, but he had never heard of it before.

He also faced—more immediately and without any question—the need for a lawyer. He had felt little confidence in the local lawyer who had appeared with him before the police judge in Hazard. But he had no money to pay high legal fees. His parents weren't wealthy. Even if they had been, he thought, his father might very well feel that Steve's defense was his own responsibility, especially since he was nearing his twenty-first birthday.

By the time he reached New York, Steve had decided what to do. He called the New York office that was the ACLU's national headquarters and was put in touch with Melvin L. Wulf, the well-known lawyer serving as its legal director. On April 4, four days after he had left Hazard, he was seated in Wulf's office. He had brought along one of the few copies he still had of his "Notes" and the Hazard *Herald*'s story about his arrest.

Wulf's immediate interest in Steve's case grew out of the criminal libel charge to which, as he declared in a letter the next day, "the ACLU's position is clearly opposed." Criminal libel was still recognized in some states at that time as a part of common law—that is, law not set out in written statutes but established only by court decisions. Only two such decisions on criminal libel had been handed down previously in Kentucky, and neither of them had clearly defined the "crime" involved. Therefore, Melvin Wulf said, "It was impossible for Ashton to have known that his conduct was considered criminal." Clarifying vague "law" of that kind has always been one of the aims of the ACLU.

The letter Wulf wrote after talking to Steve Ashton went to Louis Lusky, a Kentuckian then practicing law in Louisville and active in the ACLU affiliate there. Lusky would soon join the faculty of Columbia University Law

School, where he had taken his law degree, as a professor of constitutional law. It was a field in which he was already distinguished, especially for his victory in the 1960 landmark case of *Thompson* v. *Louisville,* a case of some relevance to Steve's and worth mention here.

Sam Thompson, Lusky's client in that case, had been picked up in a café by two policemen who charged him, before a police judge, with loitering and disorderly conduct. On the officers' statements alone, the judge found Thompson guilty and fined him $10 on each charge. Thompson claimed, when his case came to Lusky's attention, that he had been waiting in the café for the bus that stopped nearby and doing nothing more disorderly than shuffling his feet in time to the music of the café's juke box. The café owner had not objected to his presence and had made no charge against him. This meant, Lusky felt, that since no evidence of Thompson's guilt had been presented, the man had been convicted without the due process of law guaranteed by the Fourteenth Amendment.

Lusky promptly petitioned the U.S. Supreme Court for permission to plead Thompson's case there, although rarely is a case taken from a police court straight to the highest court in the land. The justices caused some surprise in legal circles when they agreed to hear it. They caused more surprise when, for the first time in the Court's history, they set aside a loitering conviction for lack of evidence. Their decision in Thompson's favor forced a change in the Kentucky law that had permitted his conviction. By 1963 *Thompson* v. *Louisville* was being widely used to defend young people protesting segregation by staging sit-ins at lunch counters, and who had been arrested for disorderly conduct or breach of the peace.

Steve's position wasn't like that of Sam Thompson or the sit-in demonstrators. But Lusky and Wulf both realized that he might have been unconstitutionally charged with wrongdoing and that his successful defense might produce a change in Kentucky's vague criminal libel law. The correspondence between the two men, following Wulf's first letter, was concerned chiefly with the possibility of that change, although it also covered such practical matters as the need to find a Kentucky lawyer willing to handle Steve's case for a nominal fee. Steve's finances were "pretty scarce," Wulf had told Lusky in his first letter.

Both Lusky and Wulf knew, of course, that if Steve were tried in Perry County and found innocent, his case would be useless as a vehicle of change. But both lawyers thought his trial would result in a verdict of guilty. Their reasoning was based partly on Steve's "Notes" themselves and partly on what they felt would be the conditions of his trial.

Some of the statements in those "Notes" were "pretty raw," Wulf wrote Lusky, "and, I would think, pretty incapable of being proved. I would think that some of the statements are libelous." But that, he added, would depend on Kentucky law—the law whose constitutionality they were hoping to test.

As for Steve's trial, it would take place in a region traditionally suspicious of outsiders. Presumably, the prosecutor would try to make sure that few jurors were strikers or their friends, or anyone likely to be sympathetic to Steve. The selected jurors might do their best to be fair and impartial. Some of them might believe Steve was innocent of the charges against him. But none of them would find it easy to take a public stand against the three influential Hazard citizens who had brought the charges.

If Steve appealed a guilty verdict to the Kentucky Court of Appeals, Wulf and Lusky also agreed, that court was more than likely to uphold it. With the possibility in mind, therefore, of an "ultimate Supreme Court review," Lusky wrote Wulf that it was important to lay the basis for that review without delay. This should be done, he said, "by framing the Federal questions accurately, raising them at the earliest possible stage, and preserving them throughout the state court proceedings."

With the help of other legal experts in both Kentucky and New York, Wulf and Lusky prepared the groundwork for a Supreme Court review. One of the experts they consulted was Ephraim London, member of a well-known New York law firm and a director of the New York Civil Liberties Union. It was London who eventually, without cost to Steve, pleaded his case before the Supreme Court. Another of the experts was Joseph S. Freeland, chairman of the Kentucky CLU's Due Process Committee. Freeland felt, as he put it, that "under the constitutional guarantees of free speech, there is probably no such crime as criminal libel."

London and the other legal experts freely offered their advice to Dan Jack Combs, the Kentucky lawyer who accepted Steve as his client. Combs, a resident of Pikeville, county seat of Pike County, was known as a friend of the striking miners. On June 21, he formally received the grand jury's expected indictment charging Steve with having "committed the malicious offense of criminal libel by publishing a false and malicious publication tending to degrade or injure" the police chief, the county sheriff, and Mrs. Nolan of the *Herald*.

Two days later, on June 23, Combs submitted a motion to dismiss that indictment on the grounds that it did not "state facts sufficient to constitute an offense against the Commonwealth of Kentucky." His motion also declared that the indictment didn't inform the defendant of "the essential facts" making up the charge against him and that its wording was "so vague and uncertain that it fails to meet the constitutional requirements."

Combs's motion failed, as all the lawyers interested in the case had assumed it would. A date was set for Steve's trial early in the fall session of the Perry Circuit Court.

Steve had been in Hazard to hear his indictment. His failure to appear before the grand jury would have meant forfeiting the bond his striker friends had raised for him.

Afterward, he went back to New York to await his trial. He spent part of the summer in the ACLU headquarters in New York "working off" the cost of the long-distance phone calls and other expenses the organization had incurred on his behalf. He also printed the dozens of photographs he had taken in Perry County and prepared the illustrated talk he would give that fall on college campuses as a fund-raising effort for the strikers. He had decided not to return to Oberlin.

The first of what would prove to be his two Perry County trials took place early in September. The result was not the guilty verdict Steve had been told to expect, but no verdict at all. The jurors had not reached the unanimous agreement required for a decision. So a second trial was scheduled, and Steve and his mother traveled to Hazard again in November, to hear once more the testimony that had been given in almost identical words two months earlier.

Steve's case involved three persons with the same last name, a common one in eastern Kentucky: Tolbert Combs, the prosecutor; Dan Jack Combs, Steve's lawyer; and Sheriff Combs, one of his accusers. They will be referred to here, whenever possible, simply as the prosecutor, Dan Jack Combs, and the sheriff.

The prosecutor was the first to address the jury of ten women and two men. He opened by quoting for the jury's benefit the charge against Steve, and he stated his intention to prove that Steve had indeed published "a false and malicious publication tending to degrade or injure" the plaintiffs in the case.

Dan Jack Combs's objective was to convince the jurors

that there was a great deal of truth in what Steve had written, that the plaintiffs had not really been injured or degraded by his "Notes," and that the "Notes" had never been published or distributed.

Each lawyer, of course, frequently objected to the statements of the other. Sometimes the judge—referred to in the court transcript as The Court—overruled an objection; sometimes he upheld it. And if an objection was overruled, the objecting lawyer invariably took an "exception," thus establishing his right to challenge the ruling before a higher court if the case was appealed.

In questioning Chief Luttrell, for example, the prosecutor asked if the police chief had seized "a mailing list" at the time of Steve's arrest. The court transcript records the following conversation:

Dan Jack Combs: I object.
The Court: Sustained. I'll let him tell whether he knows if any were mailed or not. The mailing list has nothing to do with this case. . . .
(To which ruling Prosecutor Combs took exception.)

From then on the exchange was a series of thrusts and parries between the prosecutor and the defense counsel, with the judge acting as a referee. The prosecutor, of course, was trying to impress the jury with the fact that Steve intended to mail the allegedly libelous letter. The defense attorney was trying to impress the jury with the fact that Steve's intention had nothing to do with the case—that the letters, in fact, had not been mailed to anyone and therefore could not have damaged any of the plaintiffs' reputations. The judge ended that particular exchange with the words "I'll let him say what he has done, but not what he was going to do. You can't hold what a man is going to do against him."

The prosecutor next asked the police chief whether there

was any truth to the statement that "it took three men to guard this one city policeman to keep him from being killed, as printed in that pamphlet."

"Absolutely no truth to it whatsoever," Chief Luttrell replied. "It is falsehood from beginning to end."

Luttrell gave the same answer to the prosecutor's question about Steve's statement that the chief had a $100-a-week job guarding a mine owner's house. And when the prosecutor asked if Steve could have "ascertained the truth from you about this," Chief Luttrell said, "Absolutely. He could have found out if he had wanted to."

The prosecutor asked whether Steve's statements had been "widely talked about." Again, the court transcript:

Chief Luttrell: Yes, there's a lot of people found out about it . . . and of course, naturally, it was being discussed among the people who knew it was being printed—

Dan Jack Combs: Object. This is a conclusion on the part of the witness.

The Court: Sustained. I'll let him tell who he heard talk about it. . . . Tell us somebody. Just the ones you know about.

Chief Luttrell: Well, all the policemen discussed it, and the city manager and the city attorney.

The Court: Now, you are the one that showed it to them, aren't you? He didn't show it to them, did he?

Chief Luttrell: I don't know whether I—no, he didn't show it to them, I know . . . I don't even know whether I showed it to them.

Dan Jack Combs began his cross-examination by trying to establish the truth of Steve's statements about the sheriff. He sometimes addressed the chief by his popular nickname.

Dan Jack Combs: I believe that the sheriff at this time had more deputies than Perry County has ever had in the history of the county. Isn't that true, Bud? Wasn't all this common knowledge?

Chief Luttrell: I don't know exactly how many the others had, but I know that it's been a policy if someone wants to be a deputy sheriff, why, they kind of put 'em on.

Dan Jack Combs: His deputies did carry guns, didn't they?

Chief Luttrell: Some of them did.

A little later Dan Jack Combs attempted to show that Chief Luttrell had been unharmed—had not been "degraded," as charged—by Steve's statements about him.

Dan Jack Combs: Now, you are still chief of police, aren't you?

Chief Luttrell: Yes, I am, I imagine.

Dan Jack Combs: Well, are you or aren't you?

Chief Luttrell: Yes, I am.

Dan Jack Combs: You haven't been hurt too much, have you? I mean professionally? . . . Have you lost wages? Been demoted in rank?

Chief Luttrell: No, I haven't.

"Had you seen this boy—did you know him or had you ever spoken to him before the time you arrested him?" Dan Jack Combs asked finally.

"He never contacted us to find out our side of this thing at all," Chief Luttrell answered.

Shortly afterward, Mrs. Nolan, the *Herald* editor, took the stand. The statement in Steve's "Notes" about her and the contributions to the strikers was read aloud and she was asked by the prosecutor if any part of it was true.

She answered that all the money mentioned in the statement had been spent "for the welfare of the needy people. I don't know whether they were all miners," she added, "or whether they were all pickets, or what they were, but it was all sent to the needy people—every penny of it."

"Then, Mrs. Nolan," Prosecutor Combs said, "this article written by this defendant, Steve Ashton, according to your testimony, is untrue?"

"It certainly is," Mrs. Nolan said, "and he never came to me one time and asked one question."

"Now tell the jury what effect this pamphlet had on you, and your feeling, as to whether or not it degraded you," the prosecutor said.

"Well, you know, any time the public talks about you it hurts your feelings," Mrs. Nolan said. "We're all human, and I had really felt we were doing a good work, and I know we were trying to do a good job. Of course we had a group that worked with us. I was not the last word."

In his cross-examination, Dan Jack Combs immediately asked her how much of the $14,000 that her office had received had been given to the Perry County pickets.

"All the money went to the unemployed people," Mrs. Nolan said.

"He said pickets," the judge told her pointedly.

"I don't know who it went to," Mrs. Nolan insisted.

Dan Jack Combs reminded her that during the first trial she had said that $1,100 had gone to the Perry County pickets.

And when Mrs. Nolan didn't deny having made that answer, Dan Jack Combs reminded the jurors that $1,100 was the exact figure given in Steve's "Notes."

Prosecutor Combs then put the third complainant, Sheriff Combs, on the stand. Asked about Steve's statement that the sheriff had blinded a boy with tear gas and beat him while he was handcuffed and locked in a cell, the sheriff said, "I wasn't even at the jail at the time this happened." He also denied having offered the boy $75,000 to keep his case out of court.

Dan Jack Combs interrupted to point out that Steve had written only that the sheriff had "probably" made that offer.

As the questions continued, the sheriff admitted he had been, as Steve wrote, indicted for voluntary manslaughter.

The prosecutor then asked the sheriff whether he had felt Steve's pamphlet had degraded him in the community.

"I certainly did," the sheriff said, and at the prosecutor's suggestion he described the pamphlet's effect on him.

"Well, people always looking at you as you go down the street and wondering if you really did that," he said. "They don't know. Just what they read, that's all they've got to go by . . . and this news—this publicity of this thing, scattered far and near, even all over the United States. As far as locally, it didn't hurt me too bad locally, because most of the people know me, but outside of the state where people don't know me, it's pretty rough."

"If Your Honor please," Dan Jack Combs said quickly, "there's no evidence of any publication even within the city, much less outside the state. . . . I would like to move the court to strike that portion of his testimony."

The judge agreed.

At the close of the prosecutor's presentation, Dan Jack Combs moved for Steve's immediate acquittal. "We feel," he said, "that the Commonwealth has failed to prove the essential elements of the crime of criminal libel, to wit: a malicious publication."

The plaintiffs had "absolutely failed to show any malice on the part of the accused," he said, and "they have failed to prove publication." As to the falsity of Steve's pamphlet, he said, "they said, yes, it's false, but on cross-examination, point by point, each of the prosecuting witnesses admitted that there was truth. . . . Now, there's some inflection, some interpretations, but basically everything this boy said was true. . . .

"Now, these people—they say they have been degraded," he went on. "They don't know how they have been degraded. Bud is still chief. Charlie still has the support of the rich and the poor, and Mrs. Nolan is still a highly respected editor.

"I feel that we are entitled . . . to a directed verdict of acquittal, Your Honor," he concluded.

The judge had listened to him patiently. He listened to Prosecutor Combs's arguments against the motion. Then he said he was "very sympathetic" to what Dan Jack Combs had said, and that he felt the case against Steve Ashton was "thin—real thin. But I'm going to overrule his motion," he added, "and let him put on his evidence."

Dan Jack Combs now had to present Steve's side of the case. He and his advisers had agreed that Steve himself should not take the stand. If he did, and was required to answer the prosecutor's questions, his background of civil rights activities would certainly be exposed and would be bound to injure him in the eyes of Perry County jurors. So Dan Jack Combs called Sylvia Ashton, Steve's mother, and gave her the chance to talk about some of Steve's other youthful activities. They included playing on a Little League baseball team, serving as a class officer in junior high school, and serving as president of his high school senior class.

The prosecutor, in his cross-examination, asked if Steve hadn't been expelled from Oberlin. She said he hadn't. He asked if Steve had organized a group of Oberlin students "to fight the House Un-American Activities Committee." Dan Jack Combs objected, and the judge sustained his objection.

Then the prosecutor asked why Steve had come to Hazard. Mrs. Ashton said it was because he and many other people understood that "help, food, and clothing" were desperately needed.

Prosecutor: Where?
Mrs. Ashton: Right here.
Prosecutor: How do you know? Were you down here?
Mrs. Ashton: We had a documentary that we—
Prosecutor (*interrupting*): Oh, you're just going by what somebody told you, that there was a desperate situation down here, is that right?
The Court: Everybody that saw that TV program would have a pretty good idea of what was going on down here, I think. I saw it, and I suppose a good many other people saw it.

The prosecutor asked about Steve's stay at Tougaloo, which he referred to as "this colored college," and whether or not the Ashtons had "any business interests in eastern Kentucky."

The judge said she need not answer the last question because it was "immaterial," but Mrs. Ashton said, "We have no business interests anywhere, Your Honor. We work, like everybody else."

Dan Jack Combs also put some Perry County citizens on the stand to testify about the help Steve had brought to Hazard. And Ira Kilburn, the policeman whose life Steve said had been threatened by Chief Luttrell, testified about that threat.

"In a conversation with Bud Luttrell, did he ever tell you that your life was in danger?" Dan Jack Combs asked him.

"Yes, sir," Kilburn answered. "He told me that if I didn't make a move I would be killed, and I made the move."

Finally, the judge gave the jury his lengthy instructions. He said the jurors would find Steve guilty if they believed he had maliciously written and published false and libelous statements for the purpose of bringing the plaintiffs into "great contempt, scandal, infamy, and disgrace" and for "vilifying" their names and reputations.

He said the jurors would find Steve *not* guilty if they believed the prosecutor had failed to prove that the alleged libelous statements in his pamphlet were false.

He also made a point that had been scarcely touched on before, except for a brief reference by Dan Jack Combs, and that would eventually prove a vital issue in the case. "Criminal libel," the judge said, "is defined as any writing calculated to create disturbances of the peace, corrupt the public morals, or lead to any act which, when done, is indictable."

The jurors returned from their deliberations with the report that they, like the jurors in the first trial, had been unable to reach the unanimous agreement necessary for a verdict. A choice had to be made: Steve could prepare for a third trial, which might once more result in a hung jury; or he could accept the decision of the majority of the jurors as a final verdict. He chose to accept the majority decision.

Steve was declared guilty by a vote of ten to two and sentenced to six months in jail and a fine of $3,000. But he was immediately freed on bail to await the appeal his legal advisers had long ago agreed on. His case could now move toward the "ultimate review" Lusky and Wulf had discussed months before.

During the long wait while his case reached the Kentucky Court of Appeals, Steve's Hazard photographs aroused so much admiration that for the first time he began to take photography seriously. The courses he took in photographic techniques and film production at New York University led him ultimately to a career in documentary filmmaking.

Times v. *Sullivan,* an important case that had a bearing on Steve's, was settled during 1964. An Alabama public official had obtained a libel judgment of $500,000 against the *New York Times;* the newspaper's attorneys, supported by other papers and by the ACLU, had taken the case to the Supreme Court and won a reversal of the verdict. In a unanimous decision, the justices barred libel or slander suits against anyone who commented on an official's conduct, unless the comment was made with the knowledge that it was false, or with reckless disregard for the truth. The decision even protected statements that were in error: If a person sued for libel had to prove the truth of every statement, the justices said, that "would place too great a burden on free speech."

That Supreme Court decision was cited in Steve's appeal. The appeal pointed out, referring to that case, that public officials—such as Sheriff Combs and Chief Luttrell—had no legal recourse against criticism unless they could prove it had been leveled at them with malice.

The other chief claim in Steve's appeal was that the definition of criminal libel used in his case was so vague and inconclusive that he had been convicted without due process of law, as well as in violation of freedom of the press.

The appeal failed. With three of the seven judges dissenting, the Kentucky Court of Appeals upheld Steve's conviction. But its decision pointed out that the Perry County judge's instructions to the jury had been "somewhat confusing," because he had referred to criminal libel as writing "calculated to create a disturbance of the peace." The use of those words, the appeals court decision declared, would make Kentucky's criminal libel law unconstitutional, and it therefore gave its own definition of the crime: the publication, with malice, of a defamatory statement about another that is false.

The time was finally at hand for the "ultimate review"

of Steve's case and Kentucky's criminal libel law. It was on April 28, 1966—almost three years after his arrest—that he went to Washington to hear the presentation before the black-robed justices. He sat among the spectators in the sober splendor of the courtroom. He had no role to play in this event—as, indeed, he had had no active role in his two trials and his hearing before the appeals court.

"It was an odd feeling," he said afterward, "knowing your fate was being settled by men who probably didn't even know you were there, and realizing there was absolutely nothing you could do to affect their decision."

The names of Dan Jack Combs and Melvin L. Wulf were on the brief, along with that of Ephraim London, but it was London who addressed the bench. The opposing lawyer was the assistant attorney general of Kentucky. Steve felt sure that the justices listened to London with a special courtesy that showed their respect for him.

The Court's decision was published less than three weeks later, on May 16. To Steve's satisfaction, it had been written by Justice William O. Douglas, for whom he had always felt great admiration.

It pointed out that the appeals court had adopted a different interpretation of criminal libel than had been used in the trial court, because under the trial court's interpretation the law would be unconstitutional. But Justice Douglas declared that a conviction based on an unconstitutional law couldn't be sustained in a higher court simply by reinterpreting the law to eliminate the "unconstitutional features."

"Vague laws in any area suffer a constitutional infirmity," the decision concluded. "When First Amendment rights are involved, we look even more closely lest . . . freedom of speech or of the press suffer."

The decision of the Supreme Court was unanimous. Steve's conviction had been overturned. And the kind of "vague law" according to which he had been found guilty in Kentucky could always thereafter be attacked—if not always successfully—in every state of the United States.

12

Corporal Punishment in Schools

The introduction to a book called *Corporal Punishment in American Education* tells the story of a chief of the Nez Perce Indians who was riding through a white man's camp on his way to a peace talk with United States Army officers. When he passed a soldier beating a child, the chief pulled up his horse.

"There is no point in talking peace with barbarians," he said to the Indians with him. "What could you say to a man who would strike a child?" Then he turned and led his party back out of the camp.

In 1843 Horace Mann, the famous educator in whose honor schools have been named, traveled to Europe to inspect some of the continent's schools and educational systems. Not once during his travels did he see a child struck by a teacher. So different was this from the common practice of beating children in American schools that Mann was amazed. On his return, he suggested that schools in the United States would do well to find ways other than corporal punishment to maintain discipline in elementary schools. The teaching profession rose in wrath at the thought of yielding their rods and the authority to use them. Some Boston educators went so far as to accuse Mann of undermining the standards of education and morality.

Ten years later, in 1853, the Indiana Supreme Court said:

The public seems to cling to the despotism in the government of schools which has been discarded everywhere else. . . . The husband can no longer moderately chastise his wife, nor the master his servant or apprentice. Even the degrading cruelties of the naval service have been arrested. Why the person of the schoolboy . . . should be less sacred in the eyes of the law than that of an apprentice or the sailor, is not easily explained.

The Indiana court was far ahead of its time—so far ahead that the question it posed is still being asked. Today, in fact, the "person of the schoolboy" is not only less sacred in the eyes of the law than an apprentice or a sailor; he—or she—is less sacred than a soldier or a marine, an inmate of an insane asylum or a reform school. And, according to a recent decision of the Supreme Court of the United States, a school child today is less protected against being beaten by teachers or other school officials than a jailed criminal by his jailers.

Most educators and social scientists agree that the use of physical punishment in American schools goes back to the time of the Puritans in Massachusetts. They brought it to this continent from England, where whipping school children had been a custom for centuries. (Today England and Germany and the United States are among the very few industrialized nations that still permit teachers to strike children.)

In those days, of course, people suspected of committing crimes were tortured to extract confessions, criminals were lashed for infractions of prison rules, masters and mistresses could legally beat their servants, and husbands had a right to pummel their wives. So it seemed entirely reasonable to transfer to a teacher the commonly accepted parental practice of striking, caning, paddling, or otherwise inflicting corporal punishment on a child.

One early New England town spelled out a teacher's right to use such punishment in the rules for governing its free school: "And because the Rodd of Correction is an ordinance of God necessary sometymes to bee dispenced unto Children . . . the schoolmaster for the tyme being shall have full power to administer correction to all or any of his schollers."

As the decades passed and times changed, so did ideas about the rights of individuals—except, as the Indiana Supreme Court noted, those of school children to be free of corporal punishment at the hands of a teacher. Elementary and secondary public school students continued to be strapped, switched, paddled, slapped, and not infrequently punched by their teachers or other school officials. And, by and large, parents did not object to such treatment of their children. Most parents had been brought up to expect lickings both at home and in school. They were bringing up their children the same way, and they expected their children to bring up *their* children that way, too. Violence has always been a fact of life in millions of American homes.

For many years there was no concerted effort to reduce or eliminate corporal punishment in public schools. It wasn't until the 1960s that the twin problems of child abuse in the home and corporal punishment in schools began to get public recognition. And, during the early 1970s, various organizations began to look into the problem. Some were primarily interested in the psychological effects on children of flogging and paddling. The ACLU directed its attention primarily to the legal aspects of corporal punishment in schools.

Two constitutional amendments, in particular, seemed to offer opportunities to challenge the practice in the courts. One was the Fourteenth, which guarantees due process and equal protection of the law to all. According to that amendment, the ACLU maintained, a student must be given a fair hearing and the right to rebut any charges against him or her, before physical punishment could be applied. The other amendment, the Eighth, offers protection against cruel and unusual punishment, and the ACLU took the position that corporal punishment in schools is cruel and unusual for several reasons: Schools are the only places where it is legal to punish children physically; showing children that violence is an accepted way of settling differences is psychologically cruel; and corporal punishment attacks one of the most important elements of democracy—the dignity of the individual.

Legal attacks on the practice launched by individual parents or groups of parents didn't accomplish much. One reason for their failure was that many states have laws on their books empowering school officials to use physical punishment to discipline students. And states without such legislation rely on the common law that for centuries permitted the practice. In either case, the courts generally clung to the long-held position that corporal punishment is an important and accepted tool for maintaining order. To bar it from schools, the courts said, the individual states would have to pass legislation outlawing it.

By 1972 efforts to persuade state legislatures to pass such laws had succeeded in New Jersey and Maryland, although Maryland's law allowed rural counties to continue the use of physical punishment in their own school systems if they chose. In addition to those two states, several cities, including New York, Washington, and Chicago, also banned corporal punishment in their schools.

But the anti-corporal punishment forces knew they still had made little progress. A poll taken at about that time showed that more than 60 percent of the people questioned were in favor of using spanking and other forms of physical punishment in schools.

A National Committee to Abolish Corporal Punishment in the Schools, formed in 1972 by the ACLU and several other organizations, did help identify the effects of physical punishment on children—effects such as aggression, violent behavior, and fear and hatred of teachers. But, like the court battles, it failed to change the legal situation. A U.S. district court judge in New Mexico, for example, ruled that a boy who had been paddled had not been deprived of his constitutional rights—that the school board's policy of using corporal punishment was not, therefore, unconstitutional. Another federal district court judge, in Texas, ruled that a boy's constitutional rights had not been violated, although he had been knocked unconscious by a teacher for entering the school for a drink of water after school hours.

In 1975 a North Carolina case reached the United States Supreme Court. It concerned a sickly sixth-grade student, Russell Carl Baker, whose mother had told school officials that she was opposed to corporal punishment. Russell had run afoul of his teacher's ruling that ball playing was allowed only during play periods, and the teacher had struck him twice with a wooden slat. Mrs. Baker started a lawsuit against the school officials. She claimed that Russell had been denied his constitutional rights and that it was a parent's right, and not the school's, to control the disciplining of a child.

A three-judge U.S. district court rejected both of her claims. It held that two licks did not constitute cruel and unusual punishment and that therefore no constitutional right was involved. And while it agreed that Mrs. Baker did have the right to control the disciplining of her son, it declared that right was not absolute—that it had to yield to the important right and duty of school officials to maintain order in the schools.

There was nothing novel in that part of the decision on *Baker* v. *Owen,* as the case is known. But the court did add something new. Citing the suspension case of *Goss* v. *Lopez,* it ruled that some due-process procedure is necessary before corporal punishment can be used. It said a student should be informed in advance that certain behavior may result in corporal punishment; that other less violent forms of punishment should be tried before resorting to corporal punishment; and that a second school official had to be told, in the presence of the culprit, why the punishment was being inflicted.

When *Baker* v. *Owen* reached the Supreme Court, the justices affirmed the lower court's opinion without comment. To many persons involved in the struggle against corporal punishment, this meant that the Supreme Court felt some degree of due process was required before a student could be physically punished.

While *Baker* v. *Owen* was moving through the court

system, another case was attracting considerable attention. This one originated in Florida, in the Dade County school system, which at the time was the sixth largest in the country. And while it also involved student beating, there was one great difference between it and *Baker* v. *Owen:* Russell Baker had been given two "licks" with a wooden slat; the two boys in Florida had been so severely beaten with paddles that they needed medical care.

On January 7, 1971, Alfred Feinberg, a lawyer for the Legal Services of Greater Miami, filed a lawsuit in the U.S. district court on behalf of the two boys, James Ingraham and Roosevelt Andrews. They were suing on three counts. The first two asked for damages for each boy. The third asked that the case be considered a class action on behalf of all Dade County public school students who were subject to the school board's punishment policy. The third count also asked the court to declare that policy unconstitutional.

The defendants were Willie J. Wright, principal of the Charles R. Drew Junior High School; his two assistants, Lemmie Deliford and Solomon Barnes; and Edward L. Whigham, superintendent of the Dade County school system.

Neither of the two boys could be called a model junior high school student. James Ingraham's testimony told of a series of paddlings for various offenses in several schools before the October 1970 beating at Drew Junior High School that brought about the lawsuit. Some of those paddlings had been for fighting, some for being late to class. One was for stealing a bicycle—a charge James denied and for which he was never prosecuted. A physical education teacher had paddled him for forgetting to bring some balls in from a playing field. James had also been suspended for two days for having brought a knife to school.

Roosevelt Andrews had been paddled some ten times

during his one year's attendance at Drew. His offenses, too, were varied—fighting, running, leaving class before dismissal time, eating in class, and not "dressing out" for a physical education class.

The paddling of James Ingraham that led to the court case took place on October 6, 1970. The facts are uncomplicated. Some eight or ten students, including fourteen-year-old James, were told by a teacher to leave the school auditorium stage. When they didn't move quickly enough to suit the teacher, they were taken to the office of the principal, Willie J. Wright. The students didn't need to be told they were going to be paddled.

In the trial that began on October 16, 1972, some twenty months after the start of the lawsuit, Feinberg questioned James on the witness stand:

"Who paddled you?" Feinberg asked. "Mr. Wright?"

"Yeah," James said, going on to explain that the other students had been paddled, too.

"Did you see the others paddled?"

"Yes."

"Were there girls and boys?"

"Yeah."

"Did any of them cry?"

"Yeah."

"How come you were the last?" Feinberg asked.

"Because I wasn't going to get no paddle," James answered.

"What do you mean? I don't understand that," Feinberg said.

"I said I didn't do nothing but went up on the stage by accident and I ain't going to get no paddling," James said.

James then explained that the other students had been sent out of the room after they'd been paddled, leaving him alone with Wright.

"Did you resist the paddling?" Feinberg then asked.

"Yes."

Feinberg wanted to know how James had been paddled if he had resisted, and James explained that Wright had called in his two assistants, Deliford and Barnes.

"They took off their coats when they came in," James testified. "They told me to take the stuff out of my pockets and take off my coat."

James was next ordered to "Stoop over and get your licks." At Feinberg's request he demonstrated the approved position.

"Did you do what they told you to do?" Feinberg asked.

"No . . . I stand up."

"Then what happened?" Feinberg asked.

"Then they grabbed me. Took me across the table."

Again James demonstrated the position he had been forced into—lying face down across the table, with his feet off the floor. James went on to say that while Barnes held his legs and Deliford his arms, Wright wielded the paddle "more than twenty times."

"Did it hurt?" Feinberg asked.

"Yeah," James said, adding that he, like the others who had been paddled, had cried. Then he had been told to put his coat back on and "Wait outside of the office."

When he said he was going home, James testified, Wright threatened to "bust me on the side of my head." James had ignored the threat and had gone home to tell his mother what had happened and "to see how bad I was hit."

James said his eye hurt, his arm was swollen, and his buttocks were discolored and feverish. When his mother saw his condition, she took him to a hospital, where a doctor diagnosed the injury to his buttocks as a hematoma— a local swelling or tumor filled with blood. The doctor prescribed ice packs and medication to relieve the pain and help James sleep. He also advised Mrs. Ingraham to keep

James at home for at least a week.

James returned to the hospital for a second examination on October 9 and for a third on October 14. In his testimony, he said that for about three weeks after the paddling it had been painful for him to sit.

Roosevelt Andrews, the other plaintiff, had also encountered Barnes and Deliford a number of times in his year at Drew Junior High School. According to his court testimony, Barnes was reputed to carry a paddle most of the time he was in school, and had used it on Roosevelt four times in twenty days.

Roosevelt was hurrying to his physical education class one October day when he was stopped by a teacher. Feinberg, questioning him on the witness stand, asked why he had been stopped.

"He said I was late," Roosevelt testified, adding that he told the teacher he had "two more minutes, and I can make it."

The teacher told Roosevelt that he was too late to get to his class on time and took him to the boys' toilet, where there were fourteen or fifteen boys waiting. Barnes was there, too, standing at the door, paddle in hand. One by one he made the other students bend over a urinal, and he paddled them. Then he turned his attention to Roosevelt, ordering him to bend down as the others had. But Roosevelt refused to obey.

"I told him I could have made it if he would have left me went," Roosevelt testified.

"You mean made it to class?" Feinberg asked.

"Yeah."

"Then what happened?" Feinberg asked.

When he still did not obey, Roosevelt said, Barnes pushed him against the urinal, bent him over it, and began to swing his paddle. Roosevelt struggled to an erect position, and Barnes pushed him up against one of the partitions between the toilets.

". . . and that's when he hit me on my leg, then he hit me on my arm, my back, and then right across my neck, in the back here," Roosevelt said.

"Did those blows hurt?" Feinberg asked.

"Yeah, all of them hurt."

Feinberg wanted to know what had happened after Barnes stopped.

"After he got through," Roosevelt said, "I just said, 'You're not suppose to beat nobody like that. . . . I'm going down to talk to Mr. Wright.' "

"Then what happened?" Feinberg asked.

"So he got me by my shirt and started to push me downstairs and I got downstairs and they weren't going to listen to what I had to say."

"Who were 'they'?" Feinberg wanted to know.

"They" turned out to be Wright, the principal, and his assistant, Deliford. After hearing Roosevelt say again that he would not have been late to his class if he hadn't been stopped in the hall, Wright told the boy to "get out in the front and sit down and wait."

He waited until school was over for the day and then went home to tell his parents what had happened.

Roosevelt's father went to Drew Junior High School to talk about the beating his son had received. He spoke to Barnes and Deliford, and then they all went to the principal's office.

"Was your father satisfied after talking to them?" Feinberg asked.

"Not right then, no. He got madder," Roosevelt testified.

Roosevelt's father was angrier still a week or so later, when Roosevelt was paddled by Wright in his office.

"Was anybody else present?" Feinberg asked.

"Mr. Deliford and Mr. Barnes."

Again Roosevelt's father went to the school, and again

he met Deliford, Barnes, and Wright in the principal's office.

"Do you remember what they said to him?" Feinberg asked. "Do you remember if they told him they wouldn't paddle you any more?"

"Yeah," Roosevelt said. "They said—*he* said—'If you don't want your child paddled, don't send him to school then,' or something like that. Mr. Wright said that."

During the trial, other students testified to the paddlings they had received in Drew Junior High School. Reginald Bloom told of being paddled about fifteen times, once receiving about fifty licks as hard as Deliford could administer them. Medical attention had been required in his case, too.

Janice Dean told about receiving five licks from Deliford on her first day at Drew, because she didn't know about assigned seats in the auditorium and had seated herself in the wrong place.

Preston Sharpe testified that he had been paddled about ten times during his four years at Drew, once for having his shirttail outside his trousers. On another occasion, when he was supposed to receive ten licks, he got an extra five for not assuming the paddling position quickly enough.

Donald Thomas, in his testimony, stated that Barnes carried a paddle with him during school hours and that Deliford carried brass knuckles.

Daniel Lee testified that Barnes had hit him on the hand four or five times, until, Daniel said, "it seemed like the bones was coming out." Daniel's mother had taken him to a hospital, where X-rays, according to the testimony, showed a fractured bone.

Feinberg also submitted statements from doctors who had treated students for paddling injuries. And he put in evidence the memorandum on discipline and punishment that Principal Wright had sent to all his teachers in August 1970. Feinberg wanted to show the court that the way corporal punishment was *supposed* to be handled in Drew Junior High School was very different from the way it actually took place. The memorandum said, in part:

Corporal punishment may be used in the case where other means of seeking cooperation from the student have failed. If it appears that corporal punishment is likely to become necessary, the teacher must confer with the principal. . . . In any case the student should understand clearly the seriousness of the offense and the reason for the punishment . . . and the punishment must be administered in kindness and in the presence of another adult, at a time and under conditions not calculated to hold the student up to ridicule and shame.

The memorandum added:

In the administering of corporal punishment, no instrument shall be used that will produce physical injury to the student, and no part of the body above the waist or below the knees may be struck. The person administering the corporal punishment must realize his own personal liabilities if the student being given corporal punishment is physically injured.

The gulf between theoretical and actual treatment was apparent to District Court Judge Joe Eaton. "There has been a rather widespread failure to adhere to School Board policy regarding corporal punishment," he wrote in the decision he handed down February 23, 1973, after hearing the plaintiffs' case. But he went on to say that the severe punishment he had heard described had taken place in only "one junior high school" and that the corporal punishment authorized by the school's principal and "administered generally in the school system" didn't violate any constitutional rights possessed by all the students in the system. He was therefore dismissing the plaintiffs' appeal to make their case a class action.

The judge ruled that the evidence hadn't shown a "constitutional level of cruel and unusual punishment." And he decided that neither James nor Roosevelt had been deprived of the due process of law, because the law called for no formal procedures before a school official could inflict corporal punishment on a student.

Wright and his assistants had not even had to testify in their own defense. The judge had dismissed all three counts of the boys' case without letting it come to a full trial.

Within a month, Alfred Feinberg served notice on Wright and the others that James Ingraham and Roosevelt Andrews were appealing the district court decision to the U.S. Court of Appeals for the Fifth Circuit. It was heard in that court by a panel of three judges, who voted two to one to reverse Judge Eaton's decision.

The majority based their reasoning on the cruel and unusual punishment charge the plaintiffs had made. If even one school is guilty of such treatment, the two judges held, that was enough to demand the protection of the Eighth Amendment.

The Dade County school authorities were unwilling to accept the verdict. They asked for another hearing before the same appeals court—this time before its full bench of judges. Their request was granted. And this time the majority of a thirteen-judge court voted to overrule the three-judge panel and restore the original verdict in favor of the school.

Probably the most important part of that court's written opinion was its statement that the Eighth Amendment's prohibition against "cruel and unusual" punishment refers only to criminals. The original intent of that amendment, the court pointed out, had been to protect suspects against the torture inflicted on a prisoner in order to extort a confession; only much later had it been extended to protect jailed persons against any inhuman treatment. So, the decision said, since Ingraham and Andrews had been neither punished for a criminal offense nor imprisoned, they could not claim the Eighth Amendment protection.

The majority of the court also rejected the plaintiffs' argument that they had been denied the due process of law granted to suspended students by the 1975 *Goss* v. *Lopez* decision. Suspension was a serious punishment that could damage a child's reputation, the judges said, but paddling was only "a commonplace and trivial event in the lives of most children."

Three dissenting judges took exception to much of that majority opinion. "The administration of punishment is no longer confined to a criminal setting," they wrote. "It is now employed in the public schools." And they declared that the clock could not be turned back to 1891, that "school children have a constitutional right to freedom from cruel and unusual punishment," and that "it is our duty as federal judges to enforce that right."

The minority opinion also argued against the majority's contention that paddling was only a "commonplace and trivial event" and therefore not protected by the due-process clause. Referring to that portion of the *Goss* v. *Lopez* decision that described education as a property right protected by due process, the minority asked, "Was James' loss of more than 10 days of school any less a deprivation of property because it resulted from a beating instead of a formal suspension?"

By this time—over five years after the case was first started in Florida—*Ingraham* v. *Wright* had become a *cause célèbre*, a landmark lawsuit that had attracted wide attention. And the antipunishment forces were determined to have the appellate court's decision reversed. They didn't believe a reversal would result in a ban on all forms of corporal punishment, but they did hope for a declaration that extreme forms of such punishment were violations of the Eighth and Fourteenth amendments. A petition was therefore submitted to the U.S. Supreme Court asking it to review the case. In May 1976 the Supreme Court agreed.

An *amicus curiae* brief on the two boys' behalf was submitted to the Court by the then-new National Center for the Study of Corporal Punishment and Alternatives in the Schools. The Center, as it is usually called, formed by the ACLU and various other organizations, is affiliated with Temple University and works closely with its psychology department. In addition to preparing briefs in such cases as *Ingraham* v. *Wright,* it supplies scientists to testify in court, charts the regions where corporal punishment is most brutally applied, and evaluates the educational and financial factors that can lead parents to support or object to such punishment.

When the Supreme Court agreed to hear *Ingraham* v. *Wright,* it said it would rule on two important questions the case raised:

1. Does the infliction of severe corporal punishment on public school students, without notice of the charges for which punishment is to be inflicted, and without a hearing, violate the due-process clause?
2. Does the cruel and unusual punishment clause of the Eighth Amendment apply to severe corporal punishment inflicted on public school students by school officials?

The Supreme Court decision on *Ingraham* v. *Wright* was announced late in April 1977. Defenders of corporal punishment heaved a sigh of relief when they read it. The antipunishment forces were dismayed. The Supreme Court had voted narrowly—five to four—to uphold the appellate court's decision.

Justice Lewis Powell, who had written the minority opinion in the case of *Goss* v. *Lopez,* wrote the majority opinion now. He pointed out that though physical punishment of criminals had largely been stopped, "the practice continues to play a role in the public education of school children in most parts of the country." He went on to say "Professional and public opinion is sharply divided on the practice. . . . Yet we can discern no trend toward its elimination.

"The schoolchild has little need for the protection of the Eighth Amendment," Justice Powell wrote.

. . . the public school is an open institution. Except perhaps when very young, the child is not physically restrained from leaving school during school hours; and at the end of the school day, the child is invariably free to return home. Even while at school, the child brings with him the support of family and friends, and is rarely apart from teachers and other pupils who may witness and protest any instances of mistreatment. . . . Public school teachers and administrators are privileged at common law to inflict only such punishment as is reasonably necessary . . . ; any punishment going beyond the privilege may result in both civil and criminal liability.

Justice Powell contended that the protection of due process would put an additional burden on school officials: "Hearings—even informal hearings—require time, personnel, and a diversion of attention from normal school pursuits. School authorities may well choose to abandon corporal punishment rather than incur the burdens of complying with the procedural requirements."

The minority opinion was written by Justice Byron White, who had written the majority opinion in *Goss* v.

Lopez. In what one newspaper termed a "scorching dissent," Justice White countered Justice Powell's arguments that a severely beaten child could sue for damages in a state court. A damage suit, he wrote, is expensive and time-consuming. (*Ingraham* v. *Wright* had cost thousands of dollars and gone on for more than six years.)

But even if a maltreated child won damages in a state court, Justice White wrote, it wouldn't mean the maltreatment wasn't unconstitutional in the first place. The mere fact that a person may sue "a public official who tortures him with a thumb screw," White pointed out, "has nothing to do with the fact that such official conduct is cruel and unusual punishment prohibited by the Eighth Amendment."

Reaction to the Supreme Court decision was immediate, and it ranged from fury to jubilation. The *Sun* of Corsicana, Texas, was delighted. Its editorial, headed "SPANK THEIR BOTTOMS," said:

We're glad to see that the U.S. Supreme Court agrees with King Solomon when it comes to spanking children. Solomon said in the Old Testament that if we love our children we ought to bust their bottoms when they get out of line. . . . We're glad to see the High Court show a little common sense on maintaining school discipline. We're just surprised that the vote was so close.

The *Register* of Des Moines, Iowa, said editorially, "The issue before the court was not 'paddling.' It was a beating so severe that it might well be declared unconstitutional if inflicted upon a criminal."

In Tucson, Arizona, the *Star* began:

The brass knuckles tipped a visitor off right away that Drew Junior High was a "rough" school. Given the amount of student violence in public school these days, that might not make Drew unusual. But in this case it was the teachers, not the students, who carried the brass knuckles.

The Birmingham, Alabama, *News* considered the lawsuit a waste of time:

Paddling school kids to maintain order and discipline is not the same as punishing a convicted criminal, says the highest court in the land and, therefore, does not require the protections of the Eighth Amendment.

Golly and hoo, boy. Now that is a verdict to celebrate. . . .

And as sort of living proof that judicious use of a hickory does no permanent damage, but on the contrary, is an aid to proper growth, take the case of the lad on whose behalf the case went to court. . . .

Ingraham weighed about 100 pounds when paddled for disobeying a teacher's order. He now stands 6 foot 2 and weighs 225 pounds and is gainfully employed by a Miami hospital.

It is to be hoped that the day of the silly-suit is finally coming to an end.

The *New York Times* headed its editorial about the decision "PADDLING JUSTICE." It said:

The Supreme Court, by a 5–4 majority and a tortuous bit of reasoning, has decided that school children enjoy no constitutional protection against paddling or other corporal punishment, no matter how severe or arbitrary. . . . It ruled in essence . . . that state laws provide enough safeguards for how it's done . . . and that teachers should not have to bother with pre-paddle hearings and that the kids can always sue if they are hurt too much or by mistake. Each member of the errant majority deserves at least five whacks.

There is no doubt that corporal punishment is a traditional tool in our culture's education system. But teachers are not in fact reliable instruments of justice. In both theory and practice, therefore, most paddling is an abomination of custom. . . . The child beaters ought to be on notice that they must observe procedural safeguards and constitutional limits as to who gets smacked and how hard and how often.

Alan Reitman, associate director of the American Civil Liberties Union, summed up the effect of *Ingraham* v. *Wright* on future efforts to ban corporal punishment in public schools. His summation appears in an essay in *Corporal Punishment in American Education*, edited by Irwin A. Hyman, director of the National Center for the Study of Corporal Punishment, with headquarters at Temple University.

Reitman wrote:

New cases can be brought, especially if the facts of these cases parallel the serious physical injuries noted in the *Ingraham* case. But even with the slim one-vote margin in *Ingraham,* there is no certainty that the Supreme Court will soon review its ruling. . . . So while the legal battle must be continued wherever possible, the issue must also be carried into the political arena where school boards, state legislatures, and parents must be persuaded that regardless of constitutionality the practice of corporal punishment is wrong, ineffective, and should be abandoned.

Horace Mann urged the abandonment of corporal punishment, too—a century and a half ago.

AFTERWORD

Some of the civil liberties cases we have reported in these pages took place a dozen or more years ago. Some were just being adjudicated as we were working on the book. Countless others will reach the courts in the future. And they, too—like Gault, Tinker, Ashton, and the rest—will affect the lives of many persons other than those directly involved.

The amendments to the United States Constitution defining the rights of individuals are very brief. The Constitution's authors used fewer than five hundred words to write the first ten, the Bill of Rights. No more than that were needed by the authors of the Fourteenth Amendment, which in 1868 gave Americans the important protection of the Constitution's due-process clause. Yet the interpretation of these amendments has engendered—and will continue to engender—an enormous amount of legal controversy.

That controversy is inevitable because, as we have tried to point out, attacks against civil rights never end. One attack may simply be a more powerful, or a more subtle, version of an old one, long familiar to civil rights defenders. Another may come as a surprise because it has arisen out of conditions that never existed until a few years ago. The authors of the Constitution could not have foreseen, for example, that the right of privacy could one day be threatened by the tapping of telephones or the computerized storing of millions of bits of information about citizens' personal finances, living conditions, even their opinions. The ACLU, as might be expected, is continually fighting new threats to civil liberties made possible by technological developments.

Nevertheless, it is important to remember that neither the ACLU nor any other organization can protect an individual's rights unless it knows that those rights have been endangered or denied. For every Gault or Tinker there are probably hundreds of other Americans, young and old, who suffer the loss of their civil rights without protest. Many of those people do not know what their rights are. It is for them that the ACLU has issued its many publications spelling out the rights of young people, elderly people, teachers, parents, and more than a dozen other specific groups.

The preface to the ACLU's *The Rights of Students* declares: "The hope . . . is that Americans informed of their rights will be encouraged to exercise them. Through their exercise, rights are given life. If they are rarely used, they may be forgotten and violations may become routine."

So the ACLU believes—as do the authors of this book—that it is our responsibility as citizens to be aware of the rights guaranteed to us by the Constitution, to exercise those rights, and to be alert to any attempt to threaten or deny them. We might do well to take as our motto two words long identified with the American Civil Liberties Union: Always Vigilant.

INDEX